I know of few prophetic voices to the body of Christ who match the consistency of wisdom and balance of truth that Francis Frangipane represents. His pastor's heart and biblical solidity flavor his writing and nourish souls unto health while calling us all to God's purposes in this present hour.

—JACK W. HAYFORD
PRESIDENT, INTERNATIONAL FOURSQUARE CHURCH
CHANCELLOR, THE KING'S COLLEGE AND SEMINARY

Francis Frangipane is a pastor who is also a prophet and a pioneer for our times. He loves the local congregations and the people he serves, but he is unafraid and undeterred to speak the truth in love (tough love, for sure) about Christ and the state of the Church. He has mentored me, a pioneer too, in the work of the Holy Spirit in calling pastors and anointed leaders together for the welfare of their community and city.

This book truly saved my ministry life! The topics and truths God gave Francis to write rescued me in the midst of a ministry crisis; reinvigorated my mind, heart, and soul; and reset my feet on a Spirit-directed path of service to Christ and His Church—and I have never looked back. Pastors and prayer-passionate leaders will be especially grateful and guided as they encounter the Lord and His scriptural vision for the Father's house. Buckle up!

—PHIL MIGLIORATTI
NATIONAL PASTORS' PRAYER NETWORK

I believe that Francis Frangipane is one of the most gifted of current Christian writers. The books that he has authored have appealed to a broad spectrum of Christians who have been encouraged and edified by many of his rich spiritual insights. I am deeply grateful for his contributions to my life and ministry. This volume has special interest to me since it focuses upon the need and benefits of authentic spiritual unity. I pray that God will use it powerfully to encourage His people who comprise the body of Christ to become committed advocates of the unity that only the Holy Spirit can provide. It is the great need of this generation of Christians.

—Dr. Paul Cedar
Chairman, Mission America Coalition

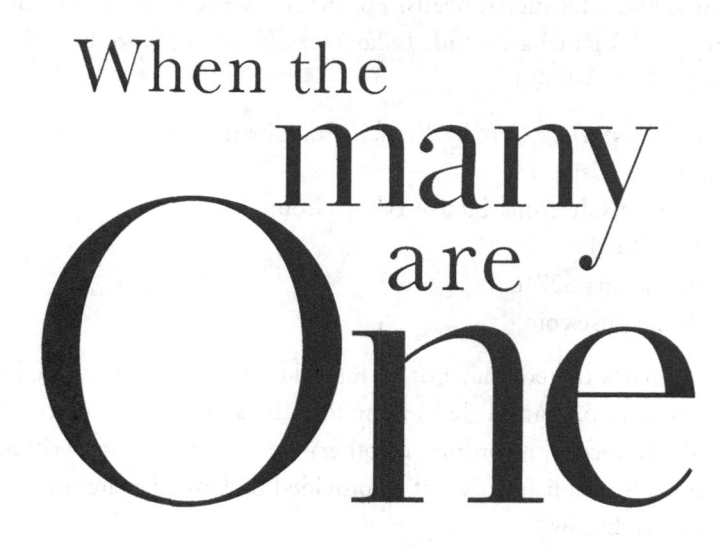

When the many are One

FRANCIS FRANGIPANE

CHARISMA
HOUSE

Most CHARISMA HOUSE BOOK GROUP products are available at special quantity discounts for bulk purchase for sales promotions, premiums, fund-raising, and educational needs. For details, write Charisma House Book Group, 600 Rinehart Road, Lake Mary, Florida 32746, or telephone (407) 333-0600.

WHEN THE MANY ARE ONE by Francis Frangipane
Published by Charisma House
Charisma Media/Charisma House Book Group
600 Rinehart Road
Lake Mary, Florida 32746
www.charismahouse.com

Unless otherwise noted, all Scripture quotations are from the New American Standard Bible. Copyright © 1960, 1962, 1963, 1968, 1971, 1972, 1973, 1975, 1977 by the Lockman Foundation. Used by permission. (www.Lockman.org)

Scripture quotations marked AMP are from the Amplified Bible. Old Testament copyright © 1965, 1987 by the Zondervan Corporation. The Amplified New Testament copyright © 1954, 1958, 1987 by the Lockman Foundation. Used by permission.

Scripture quotations marked KJV are from the King James Version of the Bible.

Scripture quotations marked NIV are from the Holy Bible, New International Version. Copyright © 1973, 1978, 1984, International Bible Society. Used by permission.

Scripture quotations marked PHILLIPS are from *The New Testament in Modern English*, Revised Edition. Copyright © 1958, 1960, 1972 by J. B. Phillips. Macmillan Publishing Co. Used by permission.

Scripture quotations marked TLB are from The Living Bible. Copyright
© 1971. Used by permission of Tyndale House Publishers, Inc.,
Wheaton, IL 60189. All rights reserved.

Design Director: Bill Johnson
Cover design by Karen Grindley

Library of Congress Cataloging-in-Publication Data

Frangipane, Francis.
  [House of the Lord]
  When the many become one / Francis Frangipane.
      p. cm.
  Originally published: The house of the Lord. Lake Mary, Fla. :
Creation House, c1991.
  ISBN 978-1-59979-529-4
  1. Cities and towns--Religious aspects--Christianity. 2. Church. I.
Title.
  BR115.C45F73 2009
  253.09173'2--dc22

                                              2009011179

E-book ISBN: 978-1-61638-817-1

Parts of this book were previously published as The House of the Lord,
copyright © 1991 by Charisma House; ISBN 0-88419-284-9.

15 16 17 18 19 — 10 9 8 7 6 5
Printed in the United States of America

How awesome is this place! This is none other than the house of God, and this is the gate of heaven.

GENESIS 28:17

Contents

Foreword by David Bryant.. xi

Preface xv

PART ONE—Cleansing the Lord's House

1   Cleansing the Holy Place.................................... 1

2   The Building Site of the Temple......................... 7

3   Obtaining the Endorsement of God......................11

4   The Credibility Factor.................................... 15

5   One Purpose: Reveal the Fullness of Christ................. 21

6   Unrelenting Love 27

PART TWO—When the Lord Builds the House

7   When the Lord Builds His House.....................37

8   Forgiveness and the Future of Your City....................... 45

9   The House of Prayer 55

10 Fighting for the Nation and the Church.....................61

11 Even Sodom.. 65

12 The Wings of the Eagle.................................... 73

PART THREE—The Anointing to Build

13 The Apostolic Anointing................................. 83

14 The Stone That the Builders Rejected 91

15 By Wisdom the House Is Built 97

16 The Dynamics of Revival................................103

17   Spiritual Authority and the Things We Love 111

18   The House of Glory 119

PART FOUR—Our Strategy: Obedience to Christ

19   Exposing the Accuser of the Brethren 125

20   God's Strategy for Our Cities....................................137

21   It Takes a Citywide Church 141

22   The House of the Lord Is the Gate of Heaven 151

      Appendix A: Chapter Highlights.............................159

      Appendix B: How Church Unity

      Has Impacted Cedar Rapids, Iowa...........................183

      Appendix C: In Christ's Image Training Institute.......193

      Appendix D: Resources 197

Foreword

FIRST, IN THE interest of full disclosure, Francis is a friend of mine.

It is more than that. There are very few on Planet Earth of whom I could freely say our hearts beat as one in our passion for knowing and exalting the Son of God. Having traveled the globe for more than thirty years, I know only a handful of leaders who share with me an unshakable hope that the Church is at the threshold of a major Christ-awakening that will transform congregations, communities, and nations. Francis is at the top of my list.

Actually, it is more than *that*. I've been sitting at Francis's feet since the early 1990s—through his writings, in seasons of private sharing and prayer together, in joint conference engagements, and through innumerable letters and e-mails. The phrase that comes to mind (with a tip of the hat to President George Herbert Walker Bush) is "a thousand points of light." To read or listen to Francis (including the book you now hold) simply "dazzles" you (I use that word carefully) like a many-sided diamond. Page after page, or (when he talks) minute after minute, I find myself constantly challenged, excited, enriched, and awakened. His God-given insights into the depths of the simplest truths often force me to revisit biblical perspectives or presuppositions I've held on to for years, only to discover that Francis has triggered in me new ways of seeing the glory of Christ and the purposes of His kingdom. Gladly, I stand in his debt—more so now, since reading *When the Many Are One.*

The day Francis sent the manuscript to me I had just arrived back from our eighteenth annual Pastors' Prayer Summit here in New York City. Each year upwards to three hundred pastors from every stream of the church—denominational, ethnic, racial, social, generational—unite here for three days of reports and prayers focused on the reign of Christ in our region. This year we spent a whole evening in what was called a *CHRISTFest* (subtitled "Celebrating the supremacy of God's glorious Son for ALL that He is, with ALL that we are"). For two hours scores of seasoned leaders did nothing but adore God's Son as the supreme passion of our lives individually and corporately—and as the only hope for the healing and redemption of our city. Returning from such a retreat, I devoured Francis's manuscript because what he is calling for here is (in small steps to be sure) what we are discovering in New York.

Our primary focus is what I call a "Christ-awakening" (which I define as "God's Spirit using God's Word to reconvert God's people back to God's Son for all that He is"). This focus takes me to the gold mine of God's truth that Francis opens to us in *When the Many Are One*. Francis is so right: the kind of unity in the body that can bring awakening and transformation to a city arises *only* when Christ is revealed in fresh dimensions *to* His people in that city so that He can reveal more of Himself and His reign *through* His people in that city. In fact, "Christ-awake-ness" leading to "Christlikeness" is at the core of the impending Christ-awakening movement many believe God is preparing for our nation: He means for us to *see* Christ together for all that He is so we can *show* Christ together for all that He is.

I could give you a hundred insights from this book that have ignited my spirit this very day—easily do so. And I assure you that for the pastors and leaders I walk with—as well as thousands of devoted disciples across the body here in NYC—virtually every-thing Francis urges would receive a hearty "Amen!"

And I join them. "Amen!" to the vision of Christ central and supreme that Francis gives us because it is the one and only neces-sary ingredient to unleash what the Spirit of God has already ordained for this hour—a citywide church in every community meant to form a base of operations for the citywide advance of Christ's kingdom. Then, in the Church as well as in the city we will approximate more and more, visibly and practically, the great everlasting passion of the Father for His Son: "...that in every-thing he might have the supremacy" (Col. 1:18, NIV).

—DAVID BRYANT
PROCLAIM HOPE!*

---

* For more information about David Bryant or PROCLAIM HOPE! ministry, please see the back of this book.

Preface

I T WILL TAKE the united effort of every Christian to win the citywide war against the powers of darkness. Our separate, isolated efforts will not stop the flood of increasing evil in our cities if we, as members of Christ's Church, remain isolated from each other. You may challenge that thought, but it was none other than Jesus Himself who said, "Any city or house divided against itself *shall not* stand" (Matt. 12:25, emphasis added).

In a universal and true sense, every Christian is part of the Lord's eternal house. Practically speaking, however, the house of the Lord is only functional as we are "built together," where the Church becomes "a dwelling of God in the Spirit" (Eph. 2:22). Therefore we have taken the liberty in this book to define the house of the Lord as that living, united, praying body of believers throughout the city where the many members of God's body become one. The Lord's house will consist of evangelicals and Pentecostals, liturgical churches and charismatics; it will be free of racial and class prejudices. We are simply born-again Christians in the city, who serve Jesus as Lord, who believe the truth of the Scriptures, and who are committed to one another as brethren.

We also believe that revival is coming. But we should be forewarned: this moving of God will not impact every city. Areas where Christians are yet divided will be bypassed; darkness will continue to increase in such regions. Indeed, in most cases, even more than the obvious resistance of hell, what will hinder revival will be the stronghold of religious pride and self-contentment in the Church.

Let us also remember with sobriety the warning of John the Baptist: "Every mountain and hill shall be brought low" (Luke 3:5). Like all rivers, the eternal river of life *avoids* mountains. Yet it flows naturally into valleys and plains. Before we will ever be truly prepared for the Lord Jesus, the mountain of our pride must come down. It is a fact worth noting that, in preparation for Christ, God placed John the Baptist in the Jordan Valley. This valley is actually the lowest place in the world. The Lord began His greatest work in the lowest place on Earth. Indeed, all those whom the Lord empowers will pass through a valley of lowliness.

At the same time, if it seems as though God has been ignoring you or that you are too lowly to be used, remember that John's message also encouraged: "Let every valley and ravine be filled and lifted up." (See Isaiah 40:4; Luke 3:5.) If you have felt like a valley amidst the apparent mountains of God, know that as you are connected with the other believers in your city for prayer, the ultimate intention of the Lord is that you be filled and lifted up before His return.

God will give grace to the humble, and together they will bring a new purity to Christianity. They will speak with lasting credibility of Christ's forgiveness; they will be examples of His love toward one another.

Yes, we are greatly encouraged, even more so than when the first edition of this book was released as *The House of the Lord*, for we are seeing a tremendous moving of the Spirit of God as He prepares the members of His Church for the coming harvest. In hundreds of cities the Lord has raised up thousands of believers who are meeting together regularly in prayer for each other and their cities. This work is God's, and He Himself is the source of our great hope. The very fact that this book is in your hands and that you desire to see the Christians in your city become one is an indication of the grace of God.

Indeed, prior to Jesus's coming *for* His Church, it is our vision that He will be revealed *in* His Church. To His glory this book is committed and dedicated.

—FRANCIS FRANGIPANE

Part One

Cleansing the Lord's House

How little we understand of the One who has granted us the unfathomable riches of His presence! We are called to be His house, His place of rest. Yet not until we are cleansed of sin will His purposes for us become clear. Indeed, it is the pure in heart who see God.

And they assembled their brothers, consecrated themselves, and went in to cleanse the house of the LORD, according to the commandment of the king by the words of the LORD.

2 Chronicles 29:15

One

Cleansing the Holy Place

WITHIN THE HEART of every Christian there is a secret place, a sanctuary we must prepare for the Lord. This holy place is not unlike the holy of holies in the Jewish temple. Not until this place is cleansed will the Lord dwell within us in the fullness of His Spirit; not until this room is pure will we truly become a house for the Lord.

BRING OUT THE UNCLEAN THING

"And it was for this He called you through our gospel, that you may gain the glory of our Lord Jesus Christ" (2 Thess. 2:14). The Lord is cleansing us for the distinct purpose of bringing His people into His glory. Out of His desire to present a pure bride to His Son, the Father is purging the Church of its sin. He is refusing to allow our interchurch relationships to continue without love. According to the Scriptures, before Jesus returns the body of Christ will be holy and blameless (Eph. 5:27; Phil. 2:15; Col. 1:22; 1 Thess. 5:23; Titus 2:14). Through new and successive levels of purity, the house of the Lord will again see and reflect the glory of God.

To facilitate this process of cleansing, by way of example we will study one of the greatest periods of restoration and renewal in the Bible: the rule of King Hezekiah. Prior to Hezekiah's reign, his father, King Ahaz, brought the very worst forms of idolatry into Israel. Ahaz shut the temple doors and persecuted the priests.

1

Those whom he did not kill he corrupted. Without the influence of a godly priesthood, the Israelites soon followed Ahaz into idolatry and unrestrained sin.

Although Hezekiah was a relatively young man when he succeeded Ahaz as king, he was God's anointed man to bring revival and healing to the nation. In the very first month of his reign he "opened the doors of the house of the LORD and repaired them" (2 Chron. 29:3). He then consecrated the priesthood and began to restore the temple. Hezekiah's first priority was for true worship to be established. We read, "And he brought in the priests and the Levites, and gathered them into the square on the east. Then he said to them, 'Listen to me, O Levites. Consecrate yourselves now, and consecrate the house of the LORD'" (vv. 4–5).

God initiated His plan to redeem the nation by consecrating the priests and cleansing the Lord's house. For this task Hezekiah had been prepared. As a young man he watched Israel's "fathers . . . fallen by the sword." The men who were not slain on the battlefield could be heard weeping in the grain fields: "our sons and our daughters and our wives are in captivity" (v. 9). Hezekiah knew only one option, one plan, was offered to Israel: return to God. In obedience, he began his reign by consecrating the Lord's house.

Hezekiah next ordered the priests to "carry the uncleanness out from the holy place" (v. 5). Before the eternal One moves visibly in power, He moves invisibly in holiness. He cleanses His house. Then the outward signs of restoration and revival, the miracles and true conversions, can come forth. If God will touch our cities with His fire, He must put that fire within us as individual believers. Everything the Almighty does for us as individuals will in time bless His Church and work to fulfill His eternal purpose in our communities. He will deliver those who are not innocent, and they will be delivered through the cleanness of our hands (Job 22:30).

Hezekiah reopened and cleansed the temple. He never stopped

thinking of Israel, but he knew in order to see the nation consecrated to God, the priesthood must be consecrated. It is significant
that he made no appeal or effort to win the nation itself; he had no
program of reform other than reinstituting true worship. The king's
focus was not on turning the heart of the people but on drawing
the heart of God. If the Lord is lifted up, He will of His own will
and power draw all men unto Himself.

Even as Hezekiah reopened the temple doors, so also in us there
is a door that we must open daily to the Lord. David wrote, "'I
was always beholding the Lord in my presence'" (Acts 2:25). Right
there within the psalmist's heart was a dwelling place for the Lord;
David was always beholding the Lord. Similarly, there is something in our presence, in our spirits, that can be opened or closed to
God. We must not assume that because we are Christians this gate
toward God is automatically opened. Jesus stood "at the door" of
the church in Laodicea and knocked, desiring to enter their lives.
We must choose to unlock this door and swing it wide toward
Christ.

Yet opening this chamber of our hearts can indeed be a frightening thing. It requires that we be open to talk to God and to hear
from Him as well. It is one thing for us to speak honestly with the
Lord; it is quite another when He speaks without restraint to us.
Therefore, the most essential commodity for stimulating revival is a
tender, open heart before God.

Is the door of your heart opened toward God? Can the Spirit of
Jesus Christ come in and speak with you? Are you defenseless to
His voice? Can you sense both His pleasure and His displeasure?
For us to become sensitive to divine realities, we must live with
the door of our hearts open. It is impossible to do the will of God
otherwise.

King Hezekiah commanded the priests to carry the uncleanness
out from the holy place. The call to clean the holy place was not an

option; it was a command. "So the priests went in to the inner part of the house of the LORD to cleanse it, and every unclean thing which they found in the temple of the LORD they brought out to the court of the house of the LORD" (2 Chron. 29:16).

When the priests entered the holy place, they entered alone; the rest of Israel was in the outer court and beyond. Here, privately before God, they were to remove those things that were defiling this sacred place. No one else had seen these desecrations. They could have remained in secret, and none except the priests would have known; but they did not. They brought out the unclean things. What was unholy was exposed publicly and removed.

From where did these abominations arise? Predominantly they were the sins of their forefathers—the traditions and offenses handed down to them from the wicked generation who preceded them. The careless approach to holiness, the unbelief toward the promises of God, and the idolatry and worship of man-made things were the products of a generation turned from God. They gave to their children, as a legacy, a society oppressed by sin and the devil.

In the new covenant temple, the Church, it is our private, inner lives that need this deep cleansing. We have inherited traditions that justify and reinforce darkness of soul within us. Most Christians have little hope that purity of heart is even attainable. The revival that will turn a nation begins in the trembling unveiling of our hearts, in the removal of what is defiled and hidden within us.

I will tell you a mystery. It is in this very place, this chamber of our deepest secrets, that the door to eternity is found. If the Father is near enough to "see in secret," He is close enough to be seen in secret as well. If He has entered us, we can, in truth, enter Him. The key to entering the presence of God is intimacy, and intimacy is secrets shared. To ascend the hill of the Lord, to stand in the holy place, we must have clean hands and a pure heart; we cannot lift up our souls toward falsehood. (See Psalm 24:3–4.) At this door of eternity we must renounce those things hidden because of shame and, in humility of soul, receive Christ's cleansing word.

THE PURE IN HEART SEE GOD

Our goal is not merely to be "good" but to see God and, in seeing Him, to do what He does. However, John tells us that he who seeks to "see Him just as He is…purifies himself, just as He is pure" (1 John 3:2–3). We can be assured that each step deeper into the Lord's presence will reveal areas in our hearts that need to be cleansed. Do not be afraid. When the Spirit shows you areas of sin, it is not to condemn you but to cleanse you.

Let me give you an example. My wife set herself apart to seek the Lord. Her cry during this time was, "Lord, I want to see You." As she sought the Lord, however, He began to show her certain areas of her heart where she had fallen short. She prayed, "Lord, this is not what I asked for; I asked to see You, not me." Then the Holy Spirit comforted her, saying, "Only the pure in heart can see God."

In the same way, the Lord desires His Church to see Him as well. Thus, He is exposing the areas in us that are unclean. If we will walk as Jesus walked, we must remember that Christ did only the things He saw the Father do (John 5:19). Out of the purity of His heart He beheld God and then revealed His glory.

The purpose of consecrating the priesthood and cleansing the house of the Lord is that we might sincerely be prepared to seek and find the leading of God for our city. This oneness transcends gathering around community projects; it is, instead, the result of consecrated men and women seeking God and, upon hallowing His presence, doing what they see the Father do.

This cleansing must become a way of life, but it does not have to take a lifetime. For Hezekiah and the people with him, it occurred in a matter of eight days.

"Thus the service of the house of the LORD was established again. Then Hezekiah and all the people rejoiced over what God had prepared for the people, because the thing came about suddenly" (2 Chron. 29:35–36). The key here is this: the cleansing of the temple was the highest priority of the king's life. When we set our hearts toward true holiness, we too will "rejoice over what God [has] prepared."

There is yet one more thought, a postscript to this message. The prophet Malachi also tells us that the Lord, "whom you seek, will suddenly come to His temple" (Mal. 3:1). As we restore God's house to purity and cleanse the holy place of our hearts for Christ, He will indeed come "suddenly" into our midst. After the Lord in His fullness returns to His house, He promises, "Then I will draw near to you for judgment; and I will be a swift witness against the sorcerers and against the adulterers and against those who swear falsely, and against those who oppress the wage earner in his wages, the widow and the orphan, and those who turn aside the alien, and do not fear Me" (v. 5).

When the Lord is in His house, He will release redemptive judgment upon our cities. Wickedness will be cut off, and our cities will be healed in His presence.

Blessed Lord, I desire deeply for You to dwell in me. I yearn to be Your holy dwelling place. I ask that the sanctuary of my heart be purged of every defilement of flesh and spirit (2 Cor. 7:1). Here they are, Lord Jesus, my hidden sins. I bring them out of the secret chamber of my heart. [Audibly identify your sins by name.] I take them out of the darkness and expose them to Your light. You have promised You will execute Your Word upon the earth, thoroughly and quickly. O God, thoroughly cleanse my heart; purify me quickly! In Jesus's name, amen.

Two

The Building Site of the Temple

T HE BUILDING OF the house of the Lord involves more than finding help in our time of need. There are costs to attaining God's best. If we want to have His greatest provisions, we must yield to Him our greatest loves.

OUR GREATEST LOVES

The Scriptures refer to two types of temples: one made of stone, which was built in Israel, and the other made of flesh, which is the Church. The first temple, Solomon's, was built at a predetermined site that God selected. Even as the Lord carefully chose the building site for the temple of stone, so He is looking at the landscape of our hearts, seeking to make us His temple of flesh. Two important events were instrumental in designating the temple site. These events developed over many years but were nevertheless a composite of what we ourselves must become. The first is found in the life of Abraham.

The Lord brought Abraham to a place of spiritual fulfillment in his son Isaac. But a time came when it was required of Abraham to choose between his love for God and his love for what God had given him. The Lord commanded Abraham to take his son to the land of Moriah. There Abraham was told to offer Isaac on the mountain of God's choosing.

"On the third day Abraham raised his eyes and saw the place

from a distance. And Abraham said to his young men, 'Stay here with the donkey, and I and the lad will go yonder; and we will worship and return to you'" (Gen. 22:4–5). Notice Abraham's last statement: "We will worship and return." We see here the perfection of faith in the atmosphere of worship. Abraham's faith told him they would both return, but it was his attitude of worship that enabled him to go up. The story is well known. The angel of the Lord stopped Abraham, knife in hand, from taking Isaac's life. Yet it was within the plan and purpose of God to require obedience of His servant. Abraham's love for God was tested and proven true.

Likewise, to qualify to be part of the house of the Lord, the first attitude we must possess is a worshiping heart; we must be willing to give to God what we love the most. For pastors, it may be surrendering personal dreams concerning their ministry or their congregations. For intercessors, it may be giving up their role of leadership in a local prayer group in order that those praying might be integrated into a larger corporate body.

In death every man ultimately surrenders all he owns to God. Those who are called to build Christ's house do so by surrendering their highest loves and their very desire of fulfillment to the Almighty. It is a death not unlike the death of the flesh. Hope of human recovery is abandoned; the sense of trust abides alone in God. Abraham offered to God his greatest love, Isaac, who was the embodiment of his spiritual fulfillment. He laid all his dreams upon an altar he built with his own hands.

Abraham was willing to trust God to fulfill His promises, knowing that death is no barrier to the Almighty. So also those whom God will use in building His house will be people who willingly surrender their greatest loves to God. Within their yielding, worshiping hearts, He will build His house.

THE FULL PRICE

The next event that reveals the "DNA" of the spiritual temple comes in the life of King David. He is standing upon a mountaintop overlooking Jerusalem; his sin has brought the Lord's displeasure upon the nation. In response to his repentance, David is told to build an altar to the Lord on Ornan's threshing floor. Although Ornan freely volunteered his oxen for the sacrifice and his ox yoke for the fire, David refused. He said, "For the full price you shall give it to me, that the plague may be restrained from the people....I will surely buy it for the full price; for I will not take what is yours for the LORD, or offer a burnt offering which costs me nothing" (1 Chron. 21:22–24).

Let us consider this fact: Ornan was a Jebusite, not an Israelite. Ornan's people were destroyed and routed from this land by David in an earlier war. The king could have taken Ornan's land at will, but instead, David pays the full price.

In contrast to typical American Christianity, here again we behold the nature of those in whom the house of the Lord is built. They are not looking for shortcuts in their service to God; they refuse to give that which is another's. Rather, these yielded souls pay the full price, refusing to offer the Lord that which costs them nothing.

It is here, at this threshing floor, that David designated the temple would be built. Yet, listen to the sacred text describe the building site of the temple. David has died, and now Solomon is completing the vision of his father:

> Then Solomon began to build the house of the LORD in Jerusalem on Mount Moriah, where the LORD had appeared to his father David, at the place that David had prepared, on the threshing floor of Ornan the Jebusite.
>
> —2 CHRONICLES 3:1

Remarkably, the very mountain upon which David stood, where he refused to offer a sacrifice that cost him nothing, is Mount Moriah, the same place where Abraham offered Isaac to God six centuries earlier.

Beloved, if we will let go of the traditions of indifference toward the Lord's house, we will be, first of all, worshipers who put on the altar of God that which we love the most. We will pay the full price to see the house of the Lord rebuilt.

Dear Lord, I desire to be given fully to You. Forgive me for offering costless sacrifices and borrowed gifts. Jesus, I want to pay the full price. I know the issue is not what I can do for You but what You can make of me. I surrender my all to You. May the quality of my life be suitable for Your house. And grant me a heart of faith and worship to bring my Isaac to the altar. In Jesus's name, amen.

Three

Obtaining the Endorsement of God

I F WE WILL gain God's greatest blessings, we must embrace His highest purpose.

THE WORKMANSHIP OF GOD: CHRISTLIKENESS

The theme of this book is uniting the Christians in a locale for the purpose of reaching their communities. Our sincere conviction is that if this happens in our cities, God's blessing will spread to entire regions, and healing to our land will occur. However, if our goal is anything other than becoming a home for Jesus, this truth will become another "wind of doctrine"; we will be blown off course again. Without the abiding fullness of Christ in the Church, we will have no more impact in the world than a political party, whose strength rests in numbers and finances but not in God.

Consequently, every serious Christian must recognize two priorities. We need to return to the simplicity and purity of devotion to Christ, and we desperately need divine intervention—or our nation will perish.

In Psalm 90 Moses utters a prayer that everyone who has had enough of his own feeble efforts should pray. In somber and earnest supplication he implores, "Let Thy work appear to Thy servants, and Thy majesty to their children. And let the favor of the Lord our God be upon us; and do confirm for us the work of our hands; yes, confirm the work of our hands" (Ps. 90:16–17).

This is a heartfelt prayer, one that is full of deep thought and candid reflection. Moses was not willing to "try something" and ask the Lord to bless it. He prayed, "Let *Thy* work appear." He appealed to God to confirm the works of his hands. What is divine confirmation? It is when the Lord works with you and fulfills your words with His power (Mark 16:20; Heb. 2:4). God identifies Himself so completely with what you are doing that He backs you up with power. It is the endorsement of the Almighty upon an individual's life.

I want to underscore that we have peace with God through Christ's sacrifice. We are not looking for divine acceptance but divine endorsement. The question is not one of salvation but of power in this life to change our world. How, then, can we truly know that we have found God's highest purposes for us? How can we, like Moses, obtain the endorsement of almighty God?

If we want our works to have permanence, then they must be the eternal works of God and not more of man's ideas. Jesus said, "For the works which the Father has given Me to accomplish, the very works that I do, bear witness of Me, that the Father has sent Me" (John 5:36). Ultimately, we only glorify God when we, like Jesus, accomplish the work that He has given us to do (John 17:4).

You may ask, "Does God have eternal, enduring assignments *for me?*" Yes, but the first "work of God" that is accomplished in us is not our work but His, that we "believe in Him whom He has sent" (John 6:29). We must abandon all hope of finding true spiritual success apart from dependent, steadfast faith in the person and power of Christ.

This forsaking of our ideas to embrace simple obedience to Christ is the "work of God." We must see that we cannot attain to the works of God unless we first become the workmanship of God. "For we are His workmanship, created in Christ Jesus for good works, which God prepared beforehand, that we should walk in them" (Eph. 2:10). At this very moment there are eternal, powerful works prepared for each of us. Yet, until we see that the Father's highest purpose is to reveal in us the *nature* of Christ, we will not qualify for the *power* of Christ, which is God's full endorsement upon our lives.

THE MYSTERY OF GOD'S WILL

If we will find the eternal works of God, we must know His eternal plan. The ultimate plan of God is stated clearly in the Scriptures. Paul wrote, "He made known to us the mystery of His will...with a view to an administration suitable to the fullness of the times, that is, the summing up of all things in Christ, things in the heavens and things upon the earth" (Eph. 1:9–10).

The eternal purpose of God is to sum up all things in Christ, things in the heavens and things upon the earth. He desires to bring the living Christ into each of us as individuals; then, as Christ-filled individuals, we can transform our congregations. Finally, from the launching pad of a Christ-filled congregation, we will see "things in the heavens" impacted and cleansed with the Spirit of His Son.

In this unfolding of the Father's plan it is important to note that the expanse of Christ must be accomplished in sequence. That is, we cannot see Christ corporately manifested in the Church until we, as individuals, embrace true Christlikeness, nor can we plunder the heavenly places until we unite with other congregations as Christ's Church.

God's will is that the Church should not be divided but united as a glorious temple, a living house for His Son. Additionally, God has blessed the Church with "every spiritual blessing in the heavenly places" (Eph. 1:3). This realm does not belong to Satan, but it is part of our inheritance in Christ. It is the eternal wisdom and purpose of God to reveal Christ "through the church"—not only to the world but also to the "rulers and the authorities [principalities and powers] in the heavenly places" (Eph. 3:10).

Satan has sought continually to hinder and delay this "summing up of all things in Christ." Yet such is our mission, and, in knowing the plan of God, such is our victory. Therefore, in battling for the soul of our cities and our nation, our victory is not in knowing how to command demons but in knowing the commander Himself. We triumph in being rightly aligned with the supreme plan of God, which is to fill all things with Christ.

Therefore, if we want to obtain the endorsement of God upon our lives, Jesus must become as real to us as the world was when we were sinners. He must become our mind, and we must become His obedient body. Throughout this book we will continually work to keep the focus upon Jesus Christ Himself. My prayer is that by the final chapters, the vision of attaining the likeness of Christ will be branded upon all our hearts and that, as sincere followers of God's Son, the Father Himself will back our lives with power.

Dear Lord, we recognize our desperate and total need of You. How we cry for the restoration of Your fullness to the Church! Forgive us for trusting in our programs and ideas; especially pardon us for avoiding You. O God, let Your works appear to Your servants and Your majesty to our children. Confirm for us the work of our hands; yes, confirm the work of our hands. In Jesus's name, amen.

Four

The Credibility Factor

I APPRECIATE AND DEFEND the origins of most of our denominations. Most were born as godly men fought against the sin and spiritual apostasy of their times. Their heroic stand preserved (or in some cases, restored) the truth of God in an otherwise dark world. From my heart, I thank God for our denominational heritage.

Today, however, the need to remain divided from other evangelical congregations is unjustified. We can remain unique congregations with unique callings and a unique spiritual heritage, yet we can also be united spiritually, and even functionally, with other assemblies in our communities.

Knowing Christ has called for unity in His Church, many leaders today are reexamining the legitimacy of division in the Church. Today's heroes are not isolating themselves from other congregations; rather, they are working with others to repair the breaches, seeking to build the citywide church on the foundation of Christ alone.

Yet our traditions of division have taken on the garments of orthodoxy; they appear biblical, but they are not. The various divisions in the history of the Church were stages in restoration meant to preserve truth, not isolate it.

IS CHRIST DIVIDED?

Every true Christian believes the Bible is God's sacred, eternal Word. Indeed, heaven and Earth will pass away, but God's Word will endure forever. What was relative and powerful in the first century ought to be just as powerful today. Listen, therefore, to what Paul wrote to the Christians in Corinth:

> Now I exhort you, brethren, by the name of our Lord Jesus Christ, that you all agree, and there be no divisions among you, but you be made complete in the same mind and in the same judgment. For I have been informed concerning you, my brethren, by Chloe's people, that there are quarrels among you. Now I mean this, that each one of you is saying, "I am of Paul," and "I of Apollos," and "I of Cephas," and "I of Christ." Has Christ been divided?
>
> —1 CORINTHIANS 1:10–13

How strange that we smugly look upon the divisions in the Corinthian church. We boldly criticize their carnality. But why was it wrong in the first century to say, "I am of Paul (or Apollos)," but permissible in these last days to say, "I am of Luther…or Wesley…or the Baptists…or the Pentecostals"?

Again, please remember, I am not suggesting we should end our denominational affiliations, nor should we strive for unity with congregations that do not believe in Christ, God's Word, the Holy Spirit, the Virgin Birth, or the Second Coming. However, I am saying that, within the sphere of the local, born-again church of Jesus Christ, divisions are unbiblical and wrong.

Paul continued his rebuke to the Corinthians: "For since there is jealousy and strife among you, are you not fleshly, and are you not walking like mere men?" (1 Cor. 3:3).

The credibility of the Church is that we are not "mere men," creatures born of the flesh without spiritual vision or destiny. We have been born again of one Spirit from above. Within our spirits is the actual spiritual substance of Christ Himself!

> Do you not know that you are a temple of God, and that the Spirit of God dwells in you?
> —1 Corinthians 3:16

We are the temple of God. Our congregations, like the stones of the temple, are to be laid side by side, building us together "into a dwelling of God in the Spirit" (Eph. 2:22).

Paul went on to issue a warning that every Christian should heed. He said:

> If any man destroys the temple of God, God will destroy him, for the temple of God is holy.
> —1 Corinthians 3:17

We have attempted to use this verse to condemn such things as cigarette smoking and sexual vices, and on an individual basis, there are obvious consequences to these sins. However, Paul is speaking here of more than the sins of excess and immoral pleasure. The apostle is warning against allowing division in the temple of God, the Church. He says, "If any man destroys the temple of God [through jealousy and strife], God will destroy him." The context is plainly speaking in regard to divisions in the Church!

When pure Christianity degenerates into divided camps of ambitious people, it literally destroys the harmony, power, and blessing of the "temple of God." The individual who brings or supports such carnal divisions in the Church has positioned himself in a very dangerous place before God. The temple of God is holy. Our unity together is holy. Our love for one another is holy, for the Father Himself dwells in the resting place of caring attitudes and loving relationships. Collectively, we are the dwelling place of God on the earth.

The warning is severe: "If any man destroys the temple of God, God will destroy him."

Yes, there are times when church leaders sin and confusion enters the dynamics of church life. So, let's make room for failings and transitions. But let us not lose sight of the fact that the living God is a God of order; He will not dwell in ruins! Because He is a God of love, He will work with us to rebuild, but He will not sanction our fallen condition with power. He will not lend His credibility to our disorder.

How Does Disunity Affect You?

When Nehemiah, living among the Jewish exiles, heard of the condition of Jerusalem and its temple, he "sat down and wept and mourned for days." The fallen condition of the temple thrust him into an extended position of "fasting and praying before the God of heaven" (Neh. 1:4). The modern Jews also weep as they face the Wailing Wall, lamenting over the ruins of their temple. Paul mourned when he saw the ruined condition in Corinth. He said, "For I am afraid . . . that perhaps there may be strife, jealousy, angry tempers, disputes, slanders, gossip, arrogance, disturbances; I am afraid that when I come again my God may humiliate me before you, and I may mourn over many of those who have sinned" (2 Cor. 12:20–21). Jesus Himself wept over the divisions of Jerusalem, lamenting, "How often I wanted to gather your children together, the way a hen gathers her chicks under her wings, and you were unwilling" (Matt. 23:37).

This mourning concerning the disunified condition of the Father's house ought to be in our hearts as well. Yet, for most of us, not only have we failed to mourn our situation, but also we have not even grasped that our disunity, jealousy, and strife are a fallen state! How far we have fallen, and how little we know it!

While the redemption of man was always motivating Jesus, remember, His most ardent desire was His zeal for His Father's house; He was consumed with it. (See John 2:17.) Building the house of God—the born-again, praying, loving, citywide church—is still Christ's highest priority. The world is His harvest; the Church is His bride. His love for the Church was the basis of His last recorded prayer: that we would be one. It is still His highest passion today. For until we are united in Him and one with one another, our testimony lacks credibility. The world will not believe that God has sent Christ if our lives are splintered with the same divisions that infect the world. (See John 17:20–23.)

PRIVILEGED TO BECOME CHRISTLIKE

There were many reasons why Jerusalem fell to Babylon during Jeremiah's day, but underlying them all was the spiritual apostasy of the religious leaders. God Himself would have defended a humble, praying city, but in Jerusalem the spiritual leaders were corrupt. Listen, therefore, to Jeremiah's fearful revelation: "The adversary and the enemy could enter the gates of Jerusalem" because of "the sins of her prophets and the iniquities of her priests" (Lam. 4:12–13).

Do we see this? Israel's enemies entered Jerusalem because the spiritual leaders were unrepentantly full of sin. O God, help us to see and accept that the future of our cities exists in the corporate relationship the spiritual leaders have with You and one another. Jesus said that any city, any house "divided against itself" cannot stand (Matt. 12:25). The place of spiritual protection of a community has its origins in the quality of life that exists in the spiritual leadership of that community: a vibrant, praying, united body of believers will move that city toward the blessing of God; a divided, sinful leadership will allow the adversary to enter the city's gates.

The path narrows for leadership until our only choice is to become Christlike in everything. However, Christlike leadership in the Church can transform the world around it! You see, our cities are in disorder because our congregations are in disorder. James tells us that where there is jealousy and strife, "there is disorder and every evil thing" (James 3:16).

Our selfish ambitions have taken our eyes off the will and purposes of God for our cities. We have become jealous of one another. Consequently, the "disorder," lawlessness, and "every evil thing" we see in our society are, at least in part, rooted in the soil of a misdirected and distracted church community.

Because of this, the Church has lost a measure of its credibility. How can we expect the world to hear our message of love when we, as Christ's body, fail to love each other? We have no right to condemn the world for its pride and arrogance when we, the body of Christ, still refuse to humble ourselves and work with the other congregations in our neighborhoods.

Beloved, over the years the world has seen many incredible ministries. However, the time of the "incredible" has passed; the hour for the credible is being established.

Dear Lord, forgive me for thinking I can somehow fake my walk with You and that You would bless and protect my falsehood. Lord Jesus, I want to be real! I want my relationship with You to be substantial! I pray for the baptism of fire to burn away the scaffolding of empty religious ritual and activity. Let Your power and Your love be the credibility of my life, my home, and my congregation. In Jesus's name, amen.

Five

One Purpose: Reveal the Fullness of Christ

THE VIRTUE OF any institution is not so much in its doctrines or organization; rather, its virtue resides in the quality of the person it produces.

A NEW AND FRESH ANOINTING

Some of you have been struggling, not knowing what God has for you. You have been through a season in which the Lord has revealed your need of Him in very dramatic ways. Jesus Himself has been near to you; however, His closeness was not merely in the way of external blessings but in the way of His cross. Yet you have delighted in this, for the way of the cross has increasingly become the way of your life.

At the same time, many of your ideas and programs that once seemed compelling now seem weak and ineffectual. Even some of your favorite Christian themes, as well as church government in general, have been reduced to a simpler, purer definition of Christianity. You just want to know Jesus. Because this breaking has been God working in you, you are uplifted.

In the midst of the changes you have been through, conviction has grown ever brighter: your goal is to see the character of Jesus Christ, His meekness, authority, and love manifested in your life. You have discovered that any other program or church activity that does not reveal Jesus is a "dead work"; although well intentioned, these dead works are powerless to transform the people.

The truth is that the Holy Spirit is preparing you for a new and fresh anointing from the Lord. Ultimately God will use you to inspire holiness in the Church and to shatter the demonic strongholds corrupting your city.

CHRISTLIKENESS OR CHRISTIANITY?

We have instructed the Church in nearly everything but becoming disciples of Jesus Christ. We have filled the people with doctrines instead of Deity; we have given them manuals instead of Emmanuel. It is not difficult to recognize someone from Pentecostal, Baptist, or other traditional church backgrounds. Nearly every congregation seems to develop a particular slant or system of traditions, some of which ultimately obscure the simplicity and purity of devotion to Christ. Submit yourself to their way of thinking, and soon you will become like them. Is that wrong? Not necessarily, but for us it will never be enough. We are seeking to be like Jesus, not men; we want the kingdom of God, not typical American Christianity.

Thus, we must be vigilant to submit ourselves passionately and solely to the Spirit and words of the Lord Jesus, incessantly reaching for the holy standards of the kingdom of God. Any focus or goal other than Christ Himself *in fullness* will become a source of deception in the days ahead.

Look at what Jesus did with common men. In just three and a half years, average men and women were transformed into fearless disciples, literally filled with the Spirit of God. They did not wince at suffering; they did not withdraw from sacrifice. These ordinary people were equipped with spiritual authority over demons and exercised power over illnesses. They were the living proof that Christ transforms people. Three and a half years of undiluted Jesus will produce in us what it did in them: the kingdom of God! Those men were as average and human as we are. The difference between them and us is Jesus. He is the only difference.

One may argue that this occurred two thousand years ago. True, but "Jesus Christ is the same yesterday and today, yes and forever" (Heb. 13:8). You may say, "But they actually heard Jesus speak; they saw His miracles!" The same Spirit that worked through Jesus in the first century is poured out upon us today. The Holy Spirit has not grown old and feeble; He has not become apostate. The Spirit is still poured out today. Indeed, the same words Jesus uttered in the first century are still "living and active" in the hearts of men today (Heb. 4:12). Has He not promised to be with us "always, even to the end of the age" (Matt. 28:20)? Jesus is the same, the Holy Spirit is being poured out, and the words of Christ still apply. We have no excuses.

The eternal One who established His kingdom in men two millennia ago is fully capable of producing it in us today. All we need is undiluted, uninhibited Jesus. All we need are hearts that will not be satisfied with something or someone less than Him.

If we divide over forms of church government or peripheral doctrines, we will miss completely the true purpose of the Church, which is to make disciples of Jesus. Some of us want pastor-led churches; others want elders. Still others will not budge without a deacon's board. A few will be unsatisfied until apostles and prophets function interdependently. Let me make it plain: God is not raising up "ministries"; He is raising up bondslaves. After we recognize that the goal is not ministry but slavery, we will begin to see the power of Christ restored to the Church.

The pattern for leadership in the years ahead is simple: leaders must be individuals whose burning passion is conformity to Jesus Christ. Is this not the highest passion of your heart, to possess the likeness of Christ? From heaven's view, the issue with our congregations is not merely one procedure over another; the concern is, will we become people who are seeking hard after Christ?

God can use practically any church structure if the people in that congregation are genuinely seeking Him. On the day before Pentecost He had but a small church of one hundred twenty people in an upper room, but they were earnestly seeking God. In Antioch there were prophets and teachers who were together in one heart seeking God (Acts 13:1). When Martin Luther was alive, all the Lord had was a dissatisfied monk, but he was seeking God. The Lord used common men and women in every revival, but first they were seeking God individually.

The outward form is not the issue with the Almighty; the true issue is the posture of the human heart before Him.

OBJECTIVE DESPERATION

We may argue church government and procedures, but the truth is that a move of God starts more "formless and void" than structured and well organized. Hungry, God-seeking individuals, meeting in a church basement or an upper room, are the ones whom God uses. The Spirit graces them with emptiness, and He pours into their hearts objective desperation. Relentlessly and purposefully they come before God, laying aside their attainments and skills. As Christ emptied Himself, so also they lay aside the privileges associated with ministerial positions and follow the pattern of Christ, taking "the form of a bond-servant" (Phil. 2:7).

They bring their great barrenness to God, knowing that true fullness is always preceded by true emptiness. They view the knowledge of their spiritual poverty as a gift from God, a preparation for His kingdom. (See Matthew 5:3; Revelation 3:17.) Is it not true that the greater the sense of emptiness within us, the stronger our hunger for God?

Those whom God chooses are "new wineskins," cleansed,

emptied, and capable of expanding with the new wine. Their hearts are containers into which the Spirit of God is poured; they swell with Christ's inner fullness. The purpose of their lives is to contain the fruit and power of the Holy Spirit.

Our approach to God should not be rigidly structured and inflexible but formless and soft. Let us become people whose heart's passion is to seek God until Christ Himself is actually formed within us (Gal. 4:19). Therefore, let us not make church government an issue. The priority is this: Will we lay aside our ideas, return to the Gospels, and obey what Jesus commands? Will we become objectively desperate in our search and hunger for God?

FIND JESUS, NOT JUST A RELIGION

In this new stirring of God, our goal as church leaders, intercessors, and members of the body of Christ is to abide in Jesus, not to elevate one denomination above another. John taught, "The one who says he abides in Him ought himself to walk in the same manner as He walked" (1 John 2:6). If we truly abide in Him, we will "walk even as He walked." Are there not a number of areas within each of us where Jesus has become more of a religion than a person?

The first-century saints had the words of Jesus, and they had the Spirit of Jesus. In that simplicity the Church enjoyed unsurpassed greatness and power. We also are returning to being His disciples, seeking to walk even as Jesus walked. This is the singular requirement in building the house of the Lord where the many are one: we must want Christ's image established in our hearts.

Is this possible? Are we being reasonable? Listen to what Jesus taught. He said, "He who believes in Me, the works that I do shall he do also; and greater works than these shall he do; because I go to the Father" (John 14:12). He taught, "If you abide in Me, and My words abide in you, ask whatever you wish, and it shall be done for you" (John 15:7). When we are aligned correctly to God's will, we will indeed have the Father's endorsement and the Son's authority.

Therefore, the Father's goal, which must become our goal, is nothing less than Christlikeness, where we become fully trained in the knowledge of God's ways. The Lord calls us to pay the same price, do the same works, and possess the exact same benefits from prayer that Jesus did. We cannot afford to compromise what God has promised or disobey what He requires. These verses confirm that when the words of Jesus are taught, and where the Spirit of Jesus has liberty, the life of Jesus is manifested. Let this become both our immediate and our long-term goal: to see Jesus Christ revealed in His fullness in the Church.

> *Dear Lord, forgive us for putting doctrines about church government and administration ahead of our love for You. Cleanse us, Master, of the effects of false religious traditions. Even at this moment grant us unrestrained passion for You and You alone! For Your glory we live and pray. In Jesus's name, amen.*

Six

Unrelenting Love

T HE BIBLE DESCRIBES our relationship with Christ in strong, symbolic pictures of oneness: He is head of a body, husband of a wife, God in His temple. In spite of these powerful metaphors, a sense of distance remains between the presence of the Lord and the spiritual consciousness of the Church. This distance is a test. Our call is to possess that love of God that reaches into eternity and brings the glory and person of Christ into His earthly house.

THOSE WHO SEEK AFTER GOD

"God has looked down from heaven upon the sons of men, to see if there is anyone who understands, who seeks after God" (Ps. 53:2).

We simply must have more of Jesus. In the face of increasing wickedness in the world, our programs and ideas have fallen short. We need God. Those who understand the hour we face are seeking Him. The wise know that Christ Himself is our only strategy and hope.

You may ask, "How does this message fit in the context of building the Lord's house?" If just one believer truly attains the hope of this chapter, that individual will change his or her world.

This message is about seeking the Lord. Our primary text will be from Song of Solomon 3:1–4, for here we find a bride and bridegroom who both are intolerant of the distance between them. The

27

bride in the passage symbolizes the Church in her deepest longings for Jesus; the bridegroom symbolizes Christ. We will start with verse 1; the bride is speaking.

"On my bed night after night I sought him whom my soul loves."

True seeking of God is born of love. Our quest for God is not a matter of discipline but of desire. It is not a question of sacrifice but of undistracted love. Your sleep is gone because your beloved is gone. You must seek Him, for such is the nature of love.

Some will say, "But I already know the Lord. I have found Him." In truth, it was He who found us. Our salvation rests securely upon this fact. But while many are resting upon Christ's finding us, His bride arises now to find Him. In the very love that He inspired, she pursues her beloved.

We must see that there is still much more to learn and discover about our Lord. At the end of Moses's life, after being used by God to confront and defeat the gods of Egypt, after dwelling in the Lord's glory for forty years, he prays, "Thou hast begun to show Thy servant Thy greatness and Thy strong hand" (Deut. 3:24). For all we think we know, we have seen but a glimpse of His glory. The apostle Paul wrote, "As many as are perfect, have this attitude" (Phil. 3:15). To seek and know Christ is the attitude of the mature; it is the singular obsession of Christ's bride.

In this maturation process there will come a point when, within your heart, love for God will take ascendancy over mere intellectual or doctrinal understanding. The bride of Christ cannot contain her longing or patronize her aching heart by saying, "I will feel better in the morning." There is simply no reconciling the passion of her soul with the absence of her beloved.

Note also there is an unfolding dimension to seeking the Lord that we must embrace. *Genuine love for God is an unrelenting hunger.* As you would die without food, so you feel you will die without

Him. She says, "Night after night I sought him." The knowledge of what her beloved has done in the past, a "religion" about Him, will provide little solace for the bride. She wants Him!

OVERCOMING RESISTANCE

There are many obstacles that hinder us from truly finding the Lord. The bride mourns, "I sought him whom my soul loves. I sought him but did not find him." Her first attempts at seeking her beloved prove fruitless, yet, unlike most of us, she does not terminate her quest. Augustine said it well: "God is not on the surface." There is indeed a "secret place of the Most High." Although hidden, it is accessible.

One common but undiscerned deterrent is the preliminary effect drawing near can have upon our hearts. We become satisfied with the blessings upon the foothills of God, but we never climb the mountain of God. We must guard against these signposts becoming our final destination. We must not be deterred by goose bumps or tears, edification or comfort. We are searching for Jesus Himself.

Let us also understand we will not find His fullness by seeking Him merely in convenient times and comfortable places. Rather, our quest is a determined, continual pilgrimage that will not end until He is disclosed to us. (See John 14:21; Philippians 3:12.) We are confident, though, for He has promised that, in the day we seek Him with our whole hearts, we shall find Him (Jer. 29:13).

CHRIST OUR LIFE

For many, Christianity is simply the religion into which they were born. For others, although Jesus is truly their Savior, their relationship with Him is hardly more than a history lesson, a study of what He did in the past. For those who attain His presence, however,

Christ is Savior and more: He is their very life (Col. 3:4). When Jesus is your life, you cannot go on without Him.

There is a story of a man in search of God who came to study at the feet of an old teacher. The sage brought this young man to a lake and led him out into shoulder-deep water. Thinking he was about to experience a baptism of sorts, the young man relaxed as the prophet put his hands upon his pupil's head and pushed him down into the water. The old man remained resolute and continued holding down his young initiate until the disciple, feeling he was surely drowning, pushed with all his strength against the old man's hands. In shock and confusion the young man burst to the surface. "What is the meaning of this?" he demanded. His teacher looked him in the eyes and said, "When you desire God as you desired air, you shall find Him."

This was the attitude of the psalmist when he wrote, "As the deer pants for the water brooks, so my soul pants for Thee, O God" (Ps. 42:1). The question here is not only of desire but also of survival. I need Him as a drowning man needs air and as a parched deer needs water. How can I exist without abiding in the living Christ?

Such is the attitude of the bride. Having not initially found Christ, she determines, "I must arise now and go about the city; in the streets and in the squares I must seek him whom my soul loves" (Song of Sol. 3:2).

This inexorable woman has risen from the security of her own bed. She has left the comfort of her warm house and now is seeking her beloved in the streets and in the squares. Pastors, be aware: not all who wander from congregation to congregation are uncommitted or superficial Christians. A significant number are honestly searching for Christ. They are asking, "Have you seen Him?"

Not only is the bride in the streets and squares of Christianity, but she is also facing the force and the power of darkness as well.

Yet nothing stops her—not her own need of sleep or her fear of the night. The love of Christ compels her.

However, again she is disappointed. "I sought him but did not find him" (v. 2).

We might think that after so valiant an effort—and in the face of the seeming reluctance of heaven to answer her cry—she would feel justified to return home. But she does not. We too must guard against becoming satisfied with our opinion of ourselves: "We prayed; we waited; we searched for God. We did more than other men." This false reward fills the soul with self-exaltation. If we truly want to find Him, we must stay empty and hungry for God alone.

"The watchmen who make the rounds in the city found me, and I said, 'Have you seen him whom my soul loves?'" (v. 3).

From her bed, to the streets, and now to the watchmen, the bride is seeking her lover. Notice that the watchmen found her. The watchmen are the modern-day prophetic ministries. Their highest calling is to find the searching bride and direct her to Jesus. While many may come to the seers for a word of encouragement or revelation, the bride is looking for Jesus. Her singleness of purpose is undistracted. She asks the watchmen, "Have you seen Him?"

"Scarcely had I left them when I found him whom my soul loves" (v. 4). This is the greatest motivation for seeking the Lord: the time will come when you find Him! You will pass your tests and overcome the obstacles; you will be secure in the embrace of Christ.

She says, "I held on to him and would not let him go" (v. 4). I am reminded of Mary at the empty tomb of Christ. The disciples came, looked in the cave, and went away astounded. But Mary came to the tomb and lingered, weeping. The death of Christ was horrible, but the empty tomb was unbearable. She had to find Him whom her soul loved!

Scripture says that Jesus Himself came to her, but in her sorrow she did not recognize Him. He said, "Woman, why are you weeping?

Whom are you seeking?" Can we see the connection here between Mary's weeping and her seeking Christ? Blinded by her tears, she supposes He is the gardener: "'Sir, if you have carried Him away, tell me where you have laid Him, and I will take Him away.'

"Jesus said to her, 'Mary!' She turned and said to Him in Hebrew, 'Rabboni!' (which means, Teacher). Jesus said to her, 'Stop clinging to Me, for I have not yet ascended to the Father'" (John 20:15–17).

The instant Mary saw the Lord she clung to Him. Love is the highest, most powerful law of God's kingdom. When you expend your energies, your nights, your heart—when you overcome your fears out of love for Jesus—you will find Him and never let Him go. Mary found Him whom her soul loved. She continued in her pursuit, remaining in sorrow until she found Him. The disciples had gone home. To whom did Jesus appear first? He appeared to the one who had the highest passion for Him. And she was "clinging" to Him.

BRINGING JESUS TO OUR MOTHER'S HOUSE

"I found him whom my soul loves; I held on to him and would not let him go, until I had brought him to my mother's house, and into the room of her who conceived me" (Song of Sol. 3:4).

You have laid hold of Jesus; you have found fulfillment. But has this seeking of God been only for you? No. For the bride brings Him to the house of her mother, which is the Church. She brings Him back to the needy and hurting, to her brothers and sisters.

We all want the Lord, but only the bride will go so far as to find Him and bring Him back to the house. I want to charge you to find Jesus. Do not merely talk about how dead your life or congregation is—find Him! Pass through your fears. Overcome passivity and lay hold of Him. The Church and our cities need people who are anointed with the presence of Jesus.

You Have Made His Heart Beat Faster

Finally, the question arises: where was Jesus throughout the time of the bride's searching? Was He aloof, indifferent, sitting in heaven? From the beginning He had been watching, actually longing, for His bride to find Him. He now speaks:

> You have made my heart beat faster, my sister, my bride; you have made my heart beat faster with a single glance of your eyes.
>
> —Song of Solomon 4:9

You are His bride. He is returning from heaven for you! The single glance of your eyes toward Him makes His heart beat faster. Such love is inconceivable. He sees your repentance as your preparation for Him—His bride making herself ready! He beholds you kneeling, weeping at your bedside. He shares your painful longing. He has been watching. And the bridegroom says, "The glance of your eyes has made my heart beat faster."

The Lord has a promise for His bride. He said there will be a fresh and overwhelming baptism of love that will surpass all our knowledge of Him. We will know the height and depth, the width and the breadth of His love. While yet here on Earth, we will be filled with His fullness.

We have many tasks, even responsibilities, that have come from heaven. However, the need of our soul is to be with Jesus. The areas of sin in our lives exist simply because we have lived too far from Him. Let us commit our hearts to seeking our God. Let us find Him whom our soul loves and draw back closer to Him!

"[That you may really come] to know [practically, through experience for yourselves] the love of Christ, which far surpasses mere knowledge [without experience]; that you may be filled [through all your being] unto all the fullness of God [may have the richest measure of the divine Presence, and become a body wholly filled and flooded with God Himself]!" (Eph. 3:19, AMP).

Lord, even now we lift our eyes toward You. Jesus, grace and truth are realized in You. Grant us grace that the truth of this message will change our lives and compel us in unrelenting love to You! In Jesus's name, amen.

Part Two

When the Lord Builds the House

Jesus said that nothing was impossible for him who believes. How is it that we are hemmed in by such little faith, small prayers, and dim vision? God is on our side! The psalmist said, "Ask of Me, and I will give the nations as Thine inheritance, and the very ends of the earth as Thy possession" (Ps. 2:8). Do not doubt. He has given nations to His Son before; He shall do it again.

I will build my church; and the gates of hell
shall not prevail against it.

MATTHEW 16:18, KJV

Part Two

When the Lord
Builds the House

Seven

When the Lord Builds His House

I**T IS POSSIBLE** for Christ's Church to be so properly aligned with heaven that the Holy Spirit actually displaces the powers of darkness over our cities. To the degree that the Church is so united with God's will, the Lord's presence guards the city: crime and immorality proportionally decline, and revival breaks out. But be forewarned: only if the Lord builds His house will He then guard our cities (Ps. 127:1).

THE CORPORATE, CITYWIDE CHURCH

"And the house, while it was being built, was built of stone prepared at the quarry, and there was neither hammer nor axe nor any iron tool heard in the house while it was being built" (1 Kings 6:7).

During these past years God has had His Church "at the quarry," shaping believers, preparing their hearts to become part of the house of the Lord. Under the hammer of the Word, many pastors and laypeople have had their rock-hard, unbending religious opinions shattered. God has been reducing their definition of Christianity to the biblical proportions of simplicity, purity, and devotion to Christ (2 Cor. 11:3). At the same time the Lord has also laid His axe to the root system of jealousy and selfish ambition. (See James 3:16.)

All across the world men and women of God are being fitted together into a living temple for the Lord. We are seeing what the Church looks like when the many are one. Burning in people's hearts is a new vision for a united Church. Together with their congregations, these servants of God are building their congregations, not upon the typical American base of self-promotion and human enterprise, but upon a substructure of humility, prayer, and a commitment to Christian love. Their singular goal is to see Christ Himself formed in the Church. (See Galatians 4:19.) In so doing, they are laying the foundation for the house of the Lord according to the dimensions of Christ, the cornerstone of the church.

How graciously these "living stones" accept and appreciate one another; how easily they are fitly joined together! The Scriptures tell us that when Solomon built the temple, "there was neither hammer nor axe nor any iron tool heard in the house while it was being built" (1 Kings 6:7). God is preparing us uniquely and individually to fit together with other Christians in our communities. This living temple, according to Scriptures, is the very "dwelling of God" in our spirits (Eph. 2:22).

WORLDWIDE VISION

It has been a primary goal in my ministry to do all that I can to help facilitate Christ-centered unity among born-again Christians. I am confident that not only is this objective possible—it is also essential. I know that there are many Christian leaders around the world who share this vision, and it is my deepest conviction that this unveiling of Christ in His Church will awaken the Father's pleasure. And when the Father's pleasure is stirred, His power to transform our families, churches, and communities soon follows.

As a living testimony of how this transformation can take place, I have included information in Appendix B to illustrate some of the redemptive effects Christ-centered unity has had in my own community of Cedar Rapids, Iowa.* At one time there

---

* Appendix C and Appendix D provide helpful resource information for local churches.

was disunity and mistrust among many churches. Today, however, there is a unified partnership of believers in the city, with many congregations working to demonstrate the love of Christ through collaborative prayer, care, and share efforts.

Men and women the world over, often of very different church backgrounds, are finding themselves kneeling in one another's buildings and praying at each other's side. Their common prayer is that the Almighty might unite them in Christ and finish the house of the Lord—cause the many to become one—that Christ Himself might heal their cities.

Given the promise of God in 2 Chronicles 7:14, if Christians are humbling themselves in prayer, seeking God, and turning from evil, why wouldn't the Lord answer their prayers? The house of the Lord is beginning to emerge upon the building site of the praying, citywide church. The time of devastation and shaping, of being hammered and cut to size, is nearly over. The day of power is at hand.

THE OBEDIENCE OF CHRIST

I acknowledge that we live in times when deception abounds. I can understand the wariness and concern that you are being asked to compromise the truth of God. Yet let us also make sure we are not confusing religious pride with spiritual conviction. Yes, let us be careful, but let us also be humble, for what we are seeking is not compromise but to *end* compromise when it comes to unity in the temple of God.

You see, our real objective is not unity but Christlikeness. We each desire to put away self-righteousness and selfish ambition and, in their place, possess Christ's heart concerning His Church. We are choosing to be the Father's answer to Jesus's prayer in John 17. Unity is a consequence to our recognizing Christ in one another. As Jesus prayed, "I in them…that they may be perfected in unity" (v. 23).

Our focus is upon Christ. So, while we were born with traditions of division, the Bible calls us to oneness with Christ and each other. Paul instructed the Church to take "every thought captive to the obedience of Christ" (2 Cor. 10:5). The areas of our thought life that are not captive to Christ are the areas where we are losing our battle against hell. But when our vision is focused upon the Lord and becoming like Him in obedience, the conclusion of what Paul wrote will be fulfilled: "And we are ready to punish all disobedience, whenever your obedience is complete" (v. 6).

It would be presumption to speculate on all that this verse means. However, it is safe to say that Paul was not warring according to the flesh (Eph. 6:12). The implication here is that when the obedience of the Church is made complete, there will be an unleashing of a new dimension of spiritual power. This unlocking of spiritual power was revealed but *not* attained in Paul's day. The provision was there in that the prince of this world was "judged," "rendered powerless," and "disarmed" at the cross—and certainly cities were impacted dramatically during the missionary travels of the early apostles—but "all disobedience" was not punished in the first century. Let us, therefore, ask the Lord Himself: Is there something yet to come through the obedient Church that will bring judgment upon spiritual wickedness and disobedience? Is there a provision in God that, through the Church, will cause breakthroughs to come to many cities?

When the Lord Guards the City

The psalmist wrote, "Unless the LORD builds the house, they labor in vain who build it; unless the LORD guards the city, the watchman keeps awake in vain" (Ps. 127:1).

Before we discuss this verse, it is important to explain a characteristic frequently found in the Hebrew Scriptures. Often the Old Testament writers communicated truth by repeating two views of the same thought. We see this especially in Psalms and Proverbs. An example would be: "With the fruit of a man's mouth his stomach will be satisfied; he will be satisfied with the product of his lips" (Prov. 18:20). The same concept is presented twice in two similar ways. Another example is: "I will open my mouth in a parable; I will utter dark sayings of old" (Ps. 78:2). Truth is conveyed using a poetic rhythm that is both beautiful and functional—a way of compressing two corresponding thoughts into one idiom.

In this regard, when the psalmist admonishes, "Unless the LORD builds the house, they labor in vain who build it; unless the LORD guards the city, the watchman keeps awake in vain," he is saying the same truth in two ways. The work of the Lord is a bridge connecting these two thoughts: the house He builds will stand; the city the Lord guards will be protected.

How can the Lord guard the city? The house of the Lord is a house of prayer; intercession brings the presence of God into the city. Let me say this another way: *When* the Lord builds the house, *then* the Lord will guard the city. The specifications of His building plans require His people to be praying, loving, and investing themselves into their cities, empowered by His anointing. When many people are one in heart and mission—one house of the Lord—it will change our communities!

Jesus confirms this in His promise: "I will build My church; and the gates of hell shall not prevail against it" (Matt. 16:18, KJV). He is stating that when His house is built in obedience to His Word, the strongholds of evil over individuals and cities will be broken.

When there is revival in a city, what happens to the powers of darkness in the heavenly places? Where do they go? They are displaced by the fullness of God's Spirit in the regional church. Paul tells us that it is "through the church" that the manifold wisdom of God is revealed "to the rulers and the authorities in the heavenly places" (Eph. 3:10). And what is happening in the spirit realm?

The Church is blessed with "every spiritual blessing in the heavenly places in Christ" (Eph. 1:3). The prevailing influence upon society in this case comes from heaven; the Lord guards the city!

When the Church is not built according to Christ's directives but remains selfish and divided, the principalities and powers have access in a greater degree to the souls of men. In such cities, spiritual wickedness guards the city.

One does not have to be very discerning to see this is true. On your next drive from the country into a city, you will notice a distinguishable cloud of oppression as you enter the city. That invisible barrier marks the influence of the ruling spirits of the community. The demonic power of that area is the "strong man, fully armed," who "guards his own homestead"; whose "possessions are undisturbed" (Luke 11:21).

But when the Church is obedient to Christ, it will be united with other believers and unstoppable by the powers of hell. Through the Church—its prayer, love, and action—the Lord will guard the city.

PRINCIPLES OF AUTHORITY

As I see it, the spiritual realm (known as the "heavenly places" in the Bible) can be occupied and ruled by either angels or demons. What decides who has the greatest influence depends on the attitudes, faith, and prayer life of the church. Although the earth is the Lord's, He put all things under man's feet; that is, under man's responsibility.

When Satan told Jesus that all the world and its glory were "handed over to me" (Luke 4:6), he was speaking a half-truth. The world has indeed been given to the devil, not by God, but by the disobedience and rebellion of man!

We have wrongly assumed that the devil has divine approval to attack our neighborhoods and our cities. Satan has access to the domain of darkness, but he can only occupy those areas where mankind, through sin, has allowed him.

Thus, Jesus tells the Church, "Whatever you shall bind on earth shall be bound in heaven, and whatever you shall loose on earth shall be loosed in heaven" (Matt. 16:19; 18:18).*

Notice that Jesus gave the same instruction for two seemingly different situations. The context of Matthew 16:18–19 deals with the devil, while the focus of Matthew 18:15–18 is sin. These realms are interconnected. The sinfulness of mankind—his evil thoughts, words, and actions—is the very shelter of the devil over our cities! If this is true, then the opposite is also true: righteousness in the Church proportionally displaces the devil in the spirit realm, offering Satan no hiding place. He may tempt, but he cannot abide. Indeed, when the Church truly draws near to God, the devil flees.

A NEW VISION

Without limiting their overseas missions, pastors are realizing the first mission field they need to support is local. Ultimately, how will the house of the Lord differ from current Christianity? Although the Lord has visited the Church with revival in the past, He will dwell in power in His house. I believe healing and deliverance will grow and become commonplace; holiness and grace will increasingly fill the spiritual atmosphere. Where the house of the Lord is built, the protection of the Lord will be felt.

Our ministry is located in Cedar Rapids, Iowa. When we first started praying together with other churches in the city, the state of Iowa was experiencing an increase in violent crime. During

---

* Some translations read "shall have been bound." Either way, my point is that the spirit realm is interconnected with the activity of man and, more notably, the Church.

this same time, however, in Cedar Rapids violent crime *decreased*. Again, we have provided additional information and testimonies in Appendix B in the back of this book. Truly, a book with just testimonies could be written if time allowed. Yet, more important will be your testimony of what God does in your life and city. As the mountain of the house of the Lord is built in these last days, Isaiah 2 says that the nations will stream to it. Our lives, joined together in Christ, are the antidote for the pain in our culture. To the degree that the Lord's house is established in our communities, lawlessness will proportionally decrease.

The time is soon upon us when, unless we are building the Lord's house, our labors may actually be in vain. But the Holy Spirit's encouragement to us is unwavering: when the Lord builds the house, then the Lord will guard the city.

Lord, thank You for Your dealings in my life. Thank You for shaping my heart to fit in with other believers in my city. O God, increase Your work in this region until Your entire Church is one body, one force, one weapon in Your hand against evil! Build and then enter Your house, Lord Jesus. Open the door of Your house, and step onto our streets. Guard our cities with power. In Jesus's name, amen.

Eight

Forgiveness and the
Future of Your City

THE REDEMPTIVE POWER of God is released when people forgive each other. Individuals, families, congregations, and even the atmosphere of a city can change when pardon is released. When such a display of grace is poured out, the activity of hell is neutralized.

THE POWER IN FORGIVENESS

Perhaps nothing so typifies the transforming, cleansing power of God as that which is experienced when a soul receives forgiveness. It is the power of new life, new hopes, and new joy. It is the river of life flowing again into the cold, hardened valleys of a once-embittered heart. Forgiveness is at the core and is the essence of revival itself.

Whenever pardon is abundantly given, there is a definite and occasionally dramatic release of life against the powers of death in the heavenly places. Observe the release of life when Jesus, on the cross, prayed, "Father, forgive them" (Luke 23:34). At that very moment every demonic principality and power that had infiltrated man's relationship with God was "disarmed" (Col. 2:15). As the spikes were driven into the palms and feet of the Savior, and as He pleaded, "They know not what they do," hell's gates unlocked, tombs opened, the veil into the holy place rent, and heaven itself opened—all because of His forgiveness. Even many dead arose (Matt. 27:51–53). The hand of God shattered boundaries in every known dimension through the power released when Christ forgave our sins.

Jesus, on the cross, "canceled out [our] certificate of debt." By His act of forgiveness He simultaneously disarmed "the rulers and authorities" (Col. 2:14–15). Likewise, when we forgive, there is a canceling of debts and a disarming of the enemy. You see, Christ's forgiveness disarmed the devil in mankind's heavenward relationship with God; our pardon of others disarms the enemy in our earthly relationships toward one another.

Consider the last time you experienced full healing in a severed relationship. It is likely that such words as *wonderful* and *glorious* were used to describe the baptism of love that renewed your souls. Can we see that forgiveness is the very heart of Christ's message?

Several years ago I met an Islamic scientist from India. Islam is a religion based on man's righteousness, and he had stumbled over the lack of "good works" among the Christians he knew. As I witnessed to him, I soon found myself in a debate concerning the credibility of Christianity. As our discussion grew mutually more ardent, two of my children approached; one was crying, the other angry.

To understand what happened next with my Muslim friend, I must explain something. When my five children were little, I developed a procedure for correcting them when there were fighting with each other. I conducted a brief "hearing" in which I judged both sides of the conflict. I ascertained who was the victim and who was the offender, and I then asked the victim to pass sentence on the offender.

"How many spankings should I give?" I'd ask the victim, who knew that next week the roles may be reversed and he or she may be in need of mercy and pardon. Thus, the wounded child would say, "No spankings." As long as the culprit expressed remorse, the result was that the kindness of the victim led the offender to repentance. The children learned the power of mercy. As the judge, I did not have to punish the guilty because he or she dropped the charges and the debt was canceled. The victim's mercy triumphed over judgment. Enmity was broken, the children were reconciled, and their friendship was restored.

While the trial proceeded, my Muslim friend watched carefully. Now, with the children happy once again, I returned to continue our debate only to find my Muslim friend say, with eyes wide open, "There is no need to continue. I have just seen the power of Christianity!"

RECONCILIATION

One of the most fundamental truths of our faith is that through Christ we have received forgiveness from God for sins, and because of Christ we can forgive one another. Someone pays the price to absorb the offense to themselves, but in so doing they release the power of God, bringing healing to souls. It may rend the heavens, as Christ's forgiveness did for us, or it may rend the heart when we forgive one another. Whether the result is spectacular or subtle, however, forgiveness is the very life of God.

When Stephen forgave his murderers, a plea for mercy with "Saul of Tarsus" written on it ascended to the heart of God. Could it have been the divine response to Stephen's forgiveness that was instrumental in transforming Saul into Paul, an apostle of God?

Consider the reunion of Jacob and Esau. Esau is known in the Scriptures as a hardened man, one who sold his birthright for a single meal. Yet as Jacob bowed seven times to the ground in repentance, asking forgiveness from Esau, a flow of life from the heart of God flooded the embittered Esau. Scripture tells us there was such a release of grace into his soul that he "ran to meet [Jacob] and embraced him, and fell on his neck and kissed him, and they wept" (Gen. 33:4). Esau's heart melted, and he chose to forgive the repentant Jacob. So moved was he that he ran and embraced Jacob, kissed him, and then wept on his neck. When we truly desire to walk in repentance and reconciliation, even a man as hardened as Esau can be touched by God!

We see this divine flow of life again when Joseph was reunited with his brothers. Having been sold by them into slavery, Joseph had every right to be bitter. Instead he chose to forgive. Note carefully the washing of the Spirit of God through these lives as Joseph was reconciled with his brothers: "Then Joseph could not control himself....And he wept so loudly that the Egyptians heard it, and the household of Pharaoh heard of it. Then Joseph said to his brothers, 'I am Joseph!'" (Gen. 45:1–3).

Joseph was so full of love and forgiveness that he actually begged his guilt-laden brothers to forgive themselves. He pleaded, "Do not be grieved or angry with yourselves...for God sent me before you to preserve life...and to keep you alive by a great deliverance" (vv. 5–7).

There was no bitterness, no revenge, no angry last word that preceded his forgiveness. There was only the foretaste of Christ's own unconditional forgiveness to every self-condemned sinner. Indeed, like Joseph, every time we forgive, we too "preserve life." We restore our brethren to wholeness "by a great deliverance."

RELEASE EVERY MAN HIS SERVANT

Forgiveness is the very spirit of heaven removing the hiding places of demonic activity from the caverns of the human soul. It is every wrong made right and every evil redeemed for good. The power released in forgiveness is actually a mighty weapon in the war to save our cities.

Jeremiah 34 unveils the impact of wholesale forgiveness upon a city, revealing what might have happened had the Jews obeyed God's call of release. The account speaks of more than the reconciliation of family relationships. It deals with the entire city of Jerusalem as well as all the cities of Judah. It reveals the wonderful wisdom and love of God in His willingness to save His stubborn, sinful people.

The story occurs at a time when the Israelites were hopelessly outnumbered. Seemingly every enemy who could carry a sword had it pointed at their cities. We read that "Nebuchadnezzar king of Babylon and all his army, with all the kingdoms of the earth that were under his dominion and all the peoples, were fighting against Jerusalem and against all its cities" (Jer. 34:1).

Is this not our battle as well? Do we not have our own "king of Babylon" with his hosts set against us (Rev. 17–18)? We see armies of demons led by principalities attacking and almost overrunning city after city. The demonic powers of immorality, rebellion, drugs, rock music, Satanism, greed, murder, and fear have all but swallowed many of our larger communities. Unless the Lord acts mightily, will we not continue to be overwhelmed by the dimensions of the battle?

Such was the plight of Israel. Yet hidden in the ways of God was a plan, a strategy that would both rout the enemy and heal their cities. The Lord called them to implement the "Year of Remission," which proclaimed complete and generous release to both servants and slaves. (See Deuteronomy 15:1–18.)

"Then Jeremiah the prophet spoke all these words to Zedekiah king of Judah...that each man should set free his male servant and each man his female servant, a Hebrew man or a Hebrew woman; so that no one should keep them, a Jew his brother, in bondage. And all the officials and all the people obeyed, who had entered into the covenant that each man should set free his male servant and each man his female servant, so that no one should keep them any longer in bondage; they obeyed, and set them free" (Jer. 34:6–10).

It is one thing to have lost at war and thus become the slave of an enemy, but it is quite another to become the slave of your brother. Yet this kind of servitude was a provision of the Mosaic Law. One's indebtedness could enslave him to another.

However, every seven years Jews who were slaves were to be released, and every fiftieth year all their original properties were to be returned. However, in all the years since the law of remission was issued, Israel had never celebrated this jubilee, and only rarely had an individual released his slaves. Yet at the time Jeremiah spoke this to the king, even with their enemies within striking range, the entire nation set about "to free every man his slave."

How does this story relate to us? Whenever any relationship exists outside the shelter of covering love, it degenerates into a system of mutual expectations and unwritten laws to which we all become debtors. As it was under the Law of Moses, so also it is in the context of human relationships: indebtedness enslaves. Obviously we do not enact the master/slave relationship, but our unforgiving opinion of the offender enslaves him, together with his offense, in our memory.

It is a basic principle of life: where there is no love, of necessity there must be law. And where there is law, there are both debts and debtors. To counter the debilitating effect indebtedness has upon relationships, Jesus commanded His disciples to maintain love among all men. For love transcends the "ledger sheet mentality"; it refuses to take "into account a wrong suffered" (1 Cor. 13:5).

How shall we deal with debts? Christ warned we would not be forgiven unless we forgave others. Whenever we are unforgiving, we are also reacting. Those un-Christlike reactions to offenses become our sin before God. To be released from our reactions, we must return to the cause, the first offense, and be reconciled. As we forgive, we are forgiven and restored; life and balance return to our souls.

In our story from Jeremiah, the Judeans did not merely forgive each other; they made a "covenant" before God. They cut a calf in two, and they passed "between its parts" (Jer. 34:18). This was the same kind of covenant relationship Abraham had made centuries earlier with the Lord. (See Genesis 15:10, 17–18.) They made a covenant with God to release one another!

The redemptive plan of God was this: If the Israelites set free their slaves, they would not be taken as slaves. If they showed mercy, He would show Himself merciful as well. The destruction of their cities would be averted, for "mercy triumphs over judgment" (James 2:13). Although they were sinners, love would fulfill the law and make all things clean for them. (See Luke 11:41; Gal. 5:14.)

Look what happened to the Judeans' enemies as the populace enacted the covenant of remission. Something marvelous was occurring in the spirit realm. Supernaturally the Lord drew "the king of Babylon...away" (Jer. 34:21). At the very moment the people were being merciful to one another and releasing their slaves, their enemy was drawn away, and their war ended! What they did on Earth was actually being done for them in the heavens.

We are just like the Judeans of Jeremiah's day. Our cities are also under attack, and no program or government aid can help us. What we need desperately are divine intervention and deliverance. We need to see the mercy of God and His convicting power poured out supernaturally on the people!

Some may say our cities are like Sodom—beyond saving, beyond redemption. This argument usually arises from a heart whose love has grown weak. Yet the first cause of sin in Sodom was a lack of mercy. God said, "Behold, this was the guilt of your sister Sodom: she and her daughters had arrogance, abundant food, and careless ease, but she did not help the poor and the needy. Thus they were haughty and committed abominations before Me. Therefore I removed them when I saw it" (Ezek. 16:49–50).

This prophecy concerning Sodom came from Ezekiel, who was Jeremiah's contemporary. He was probably speaking to many of the same people who later released their slaves. The root sin, the cause of Sodom's wickedness, was not perversity but selfishness. It was a city full of wealth but without mercy, refusing to help the poor and needy. Thus, they went on to commit abominations before the Lord. Any society that hardens its heart toward mercy opens its heart toward hell. But when a people become merciful, mercy is allotted to them.

The appeal of God is that we return to love and forgiveness. The Israelites, like the Sodomites, had fallen far short of the Lord's standard of righteousness, as we have done also. Yet, for all their sins, God had one more plan, one more divine alternative that might have completely changed the end of the Book of Jeremiah and brought lasting deliverance. It was pure, and it was simple. The Lord called for a covenant of forgiveness; His plan was to flood the heavenlies with mercy. The very mercy the Judeans were giving to each other would pave the way for God to show mercy toward them, and it worked: the king of Babylon, his armies, and every one of Israel's enemies left the nation!

THEY FELL FROM GRACE

The Lord gave the Judeans one last opportunity, but when their enemies left and the pressure upon them abated, they did something terrible. Instead of maintaining their mercy, they brought their brothers back into slavery.

"But afterward they turned around and took back the male servants and the female servants, whom they had set free, and brought them into subjection for male servants and for female servants" (Jer. 34:11). Under the fear of death they released their slaves. Now with the threat of death removed, they returned to their selfishness. We need to understand that where there is a decrease of love, there will be an increase of demonic activity in our relationships. The Jews released their slaves, and the enemy left. But like so many of us, when the pressure was removed, they returned to their sin: they took back their slaves.

"Therefore thus says the LORD, 'You have not obeyed Me in proclaiming release each man to his brother, and each man to his neighbor. Behold…I will give [you] into the hand of [your] enemies, and into the hand of those who seek [your] life, and into the hand of the army of the king of Babylon which has gone away from you. Behold, I am going to command,' declares the LORD, 'and I will bring them back to this city; and they shall fight against it and take it'" (vv. 17–22). The Lord gave them exactly what they gave each other. They made their brethren slaves; their enemies in turn made them slaves. It is ironic that when Israel was finally carried off into Babylon, a number of these very slaves were left in the land. Many of the individuals who had been reenslaved were assigned the properties of their former masters.

But do not be mistaken. As the Book of Lamentations testifies, this was no happy ending. However, for us the final outcome of the war against our cities is yet to be written. There is still time to flood the heavens with the mercies of God. If there is citywide repentance for unforgiveness, even "Esaus" will fall weeping upon the necks of their brothers. If there is a canceling of debts, deliverance can come as it did to Joseph's brothers, even to those who are guilty of betrayal. Wherever love prevails, the strongholds of hell will be torn down, and the spiritual armies surrounding our cities will be disarmed.

This release of divine power is resident even now in our capacity to set one another free from indebtedness. All we must do is forgive our debtors and maintain the attitude of forgiveness. As we release each other, God Himself will begin to release our brethren, our congregations, and ultimately our cities. It is up to us, as individuals, to flood the spirit realms with mercy. For whatever we loose on Earth will be loosed and given back to us in the heavenlies.

Father, we have sinned against You and against our brethren. By our lack of mercy and the hardness of our hearts toward our brethren, we have allowed the devil access to our congregations and to our cities; we have brought judgment to our land. Forgive us, Lord! In all sincerity we make a covenant of forgiveness with You and all men. We choose, as did Jesus, to absorb the debt unto ourselves and free one another. As we release one another, liberate us from the grip of our enemy. As we show mercy, pour Your mercy upon our cities! In Jesus's name, amen.

Nine

The House of Prayer

To reach our cities, Christ must reach His Church. He
must convict our hearts of the arrogance and pride, the jealousy and selfish ambition that have clouded our vision. We
must be cleansed of these sins so Jesus can unite us against evil.

REVIVAL FOLLOWS OBEDIENCE

"And when He approached, He saw the city and wept over it"
(Luke 19:41). If Jesus came today and gazed upon His Church in
its carnality and division, if He probed into our prayerlessness and
lack of outreach, would tears flood His eyes over our cities, even as
He wept over Jerusalem? I tell you, He would weep over our cities
as well.

Even now Christ's hands are extended in love toward our congregations and our cities. Knowing we cannot win the citywide war as
isolated, individual congregations, Jesus longs to bring us together
for prayer. He said, "How often I wanted to gather your children
together, just as a hen gathers her brood under her wings, and you
would not have it!" (Luke 13:34).

Please hear Christ's heart. He said, "How often..." He sought
to unite His people! Time and again He has called us to humble
ourselves and in united, heartfelt prayer allow Him to heal our
land. But Jesus says, "You would not have it!" The lack of blessing
in our cities is not God's fault, nor is it only because of the sins of

55

the world. A number of our national problems are because we as the Church have been caught up in our own agendas and programs. We have disdained Christ's call to obedience and prayer.

Maybe we are waiting for God to do something to unite us. Perhaps we are waiting for revival before we truly obey Him. We must see that revival follows obedience, not obedience after revival.

Indeed, this message is another occasion of Christ's love seeking to gather us together beneath His wings. The question is not, will there be revival? Rather, the challenge is, when will we obey Him that revival might come? Our dilemma is not, will the Lord bless His Church, but when will the believing Christians obey their Lord and join together for prayer?

THE HOUR OF OUR VISITATION

God has a purpose for this country that the enemy wants to stop. Even in the midst of our fallen condition, and while many are warning of impending judgments, the Lord repeats to us what He said to Jerusalem. "If you had known in this day, even you, the things which make for peace!" (Luke 19:42). There are things that make for peace, even in our cities and in our generation. When Jesus spoke these words, the Jews were about to be destroyed! But even in the anticipation of coming destruction, He said there were things that would turn the city from evil and bring it into peace.

What were those things? We can see them more clearly if we note that immediately after Jesus warned Jerusalem of her fate, He entered the temple and began to cast out those who were selling wares, saying to them, "It is written, 'And My house shall be a house of prayer' ['for all the nations,' Mark 11:17], but you have made it a robbers' den" (Luke 19:46).

Jesus rebuked the Jews because they had made His Father's house a house of merchandise. Let us ask ourselves: Are we guilty of merchandising the gospel? As congregations, do we sometimes merchandise our spiritual gifts—tongues and healing and prophecy? Do we peddle our evangelism and children's programs or our youth groups and home fellowships? God gave these differences to enhance us, while Satan uses them to divide us.

It certainly is not wrong to present such programs under the anointing of the Lord. What is wrong is to market our uniqueness as a commodity to lure people from one congregation to another. Christ said His Father's house would not be a house of merchandise but a house of prayer. Corporate, heartfelt, citywide prayer for our communities and our nation is the most essential dynamic for seeing our society turned and our cities redeemed.

You say it will take more than prayer. Yes, it will take repentance and humility and, above all else, a return to the person and words of Jesus. But our cities are not worse than Nineveh. When Nineveh humbled itself, repented, and prayed, destruction was averted.

The House of Prayer

You may feel your community is relatively safe, that the oppression upon our land does not concern you. Your optimism is a delusion. Unless there is a buffer of prayer and aggressive Christianity in your town, it will only be a matter of time before it is invaded by the advancing flood of evil.

Jesus is seeking to bring His Church to the place where it becomes, literally, a house of prayer. The Lord will test the endurance of this newly praying Church, but gradually the power of God will be released in the cities of prayer. The extraordinary presence of the living Christ will make miracles seem ordinary. Faith will once again rest on the demonstration of the Spirit and not upon the wisdom of man; multitudes will be genuinely saved.

You see, there are things that make for peace. Pastors and their congregations must repent of the independence, spiritual pride, and insecurities that have kept them isolated from each other. God has wonderful, awesome plans for our cities. But the substructure of these "things that make for peace" is the citywide church becoming a house of prayer.

Jesus said that any house or city divided against itself shall not stand. It cannot stand. The only way we can stand victorious before our enemies is if we kneel humbly before our Lord together.

Will Your City Become Darkness or Light?

As the return of Christ draws near, God will release a wave of revival that will enable entire cities, and in some cases even nations, to turn to the Lord. At the same time, there will be many more cities and nations that will not turn to Him. In fact, communities will ally themselves so thoroughly with the powers of evil that a visible darkness, as in Egypt just prior to the Exodus, will actually settle upon them (Isa. 60:1–3). Even now, many large cities in the United States and Europe stand in the balance as to whether or not they will turn toward God or become places of utter darkness, great despair, and destruction.

Before we presumptuously judge these cities, however, let us realize again that the deciding factor in God's judgment is not the sin of the world but sin in the Church. Judgment begins first "with the household of God" (1 Pet. 4:17). The direction of each individual city, for the most part, will rest upon the condition of the *church* in that city.

If the congregations in the city are united, praying together and warring side by side against evil, there will be hope for that area. If there is jealousy and selfish ambition in this corporate body of believers, there will be no successful strategies against evil or barriers against the increase of wickedness. We must understand: *God has placed the responsibility for our cities upon our shoulders!*

If you are a pastor, see if the Lord isn't calling you to contact other pastors, even just one or two, on a weekly basis. Let the Lord lead you to others, without pressuring anyone to join your prayer time. God will add to this, and following His leading and "divine connections" with others is a joy.

If you are an intercessor, we encourage you to gather other intercessors and pray for the end of unscriptural divisions. Pray for the pastors and other ministries in your cities.

Let us persevere in prayer not only until we know "the things which make for peace," but also until we are united as God's house of prayer.

> *Dear Lord, I want my city to become a city of light and our congregations to be known as houses of prayer. Forgive us where we have disobeyed and failed You, and let revival come to this city. I don't want to miss the hour of Your visitation. Amen.*

Ten

Fighting for the Nation and the Church

G OD CAN OVERCOME evil in either of two ways. He can eradicate wickedness with destructive judgments, as in the case of Sodom and Gomorrah, or He can overcome evil with good. When the Lord determines to act in the way of destructive judgments, it is as a last resort. The Father's first choice is always to move in mercy. In the heart of God, "mercy triumphs over judgment" (James 2:13).

MERCY TRIUMPHS OVER JUDGMENT

"Do not be overcome by evil, but overcome evil with good" (Rom. 12:21). Evil can be overcome with good, but to do so God must use the Church. Since the very nature of God is love, redemptive mercy is the ultimate motive behind all His actions. If we will truly please God, this must become our motive as well.

"'Do I have any pleasure in the death of the wicked,' declares the Lord GOD, 'rather than that he should turn from his ways and live?'" (Ezek. 18:23). Even in the most severe judgments, the mercy of God always seems to be revealed in miraculous ways. Although calamities will become more devastating before the return of Christ, we must be assured of this: even in His wrath God is always remembering mercy. (See Habakkuk 3:2.)

The first choice of God, however, is to bring mercy *before* destructive judgments fall. His vehicle of mercy is the body of Christ. It is with this motive in His mind that the Holy Spirit desires to build the house of the Lord. The righteousness and sanctification that the living Church produces in a society can literally preserve that society from much of the evil that might otherwise destroy it.

If we do not rise to this hour, I believe terrible consequences are inevitable. Far more than our worst fears will be realized. We cannot imagine what life will be like when plagues come and gangs of lawless, starving individuals rampage through cities, destroying whatever remains of stability. I am not an alarmist, but multitudes are experiencing the beginnings of these things even now in our large inner cities. The breakdown of law and order is already at hand. Many districts have become war zones. There is only one answer, and that is the Church. We are at war, and to win this war we must be united.

THOSE WHO KNOW THEIR GOD

In Matthew 24 Jesus speaks of the last days. So terrible is this period that He warns, "Unless those days had been cut short, no life would have been saved" (v. 22). The seriousness of this final hour is a dividing line that finds Christians encamped on either side: some believing in a pretribulation rapture and others leaning toward a posttribulation rapture. After listening to arguments on both sides and seeing the sincerity (yet inflexibility) of many in both camps, my conclusion is that I should focus on the bigger picture: we are not preparing merely for *what* is going to happen but also for *who* is coming. The bride is not making herself ready for a "date" but a marriage. If we are fully given to knowing Christ intimately, not only will we enjoy His presence, but we will also gain spiritual strength for whatever the future holds!

The key, therefore, to living victoriously in the last days is not knowing only timetables but also knowing God. Daniel foretold that, in the midst of worldwide distress, those who "know their God will display strength and take action" (Dan. 11:32). From a position of knowing the heart and nature of God, in the midst of great difficulties we will "display strength and take action."

When we consider the wrath of God, it is right that destructive images come to our minds, for such must come upon the whole world. However, Isaiah 61 gives us clear insight into the purpose of "the day of vengeance of our God." It is to "comfort all who mourn, to grant those who mourn in Zion, giving them a garland instead of ashes...the mantle of praise instead of a spirit of fainting" (vv. 2–3).

The first phase of God's "vengeance" upon the world is aimed at releasing His elect from oppression. But God does not stop there. His grace continues. Taking these very individuals who were fainting under their enemies' oppression, He raises them up to spiritual maturity. "So they will be called oaks of righteousness, the planting of the LORD, that He may be glorified" (v. 3).

You see, as God's anger is released against His spiritual enemies, I believe we will see days of great deliverance and release for the people of God. I believe that where they have suffered most from personal defeat, in those very areas God will enable people to walk in victory. Ultimately these oaks of righteousness will advance the very power of redemption that the Holy Spirit worked in them to people around them, even transforming cities!

"Then they will rebuild the ancient ruins, they will raise up the former devastations, and they will repair the ruined cities, the desolations of many generations" (v. 4).

For everyone who shares a true yearning for the righteousness of God, and for each soul who earnestly desires to be like Jesus, the day of God's vengeance is your hour of fulfillment! Are we in a time of anointed release of the Church to see the "ancient ruins" of God's house rebuilt and the "ruined cities," the "desolations of many generations," repaired?

Whether this is that unique time or not remains to be seen, but I would like to remind you that in difficult times the Church has consistently been God's tool to bring healing to the nations. Whether it was with William Booth or John and Charles Wesley in England, Martin Luther in Germany, or Francis of Assisi in Italy, it has always been *through the elect* that the Lord has impacted and transformed society. The issue need not even be End Time events; *today* the need is great enough to call the elect of God to "display strength and take action."

Who are the elect? The elect have been, at various times, Jews, Romans, Germans, Englishmen, Americans, Chinese—persons of any nationality who heard the heart of God, overcame the unbelief and discouragement of those around them, and literally moved their world toward heaven.

Remember this: the Lord's first choice is always to extend mercy to our cities and turn them from the path of ruin; mercy triumphs over judgment. To do so He needs us. The answer to the present condition in our nation is not new government programs or new policies, but it is New Testament Christianity—oaks of righteousness that are empowered with the redemptive mercy of God.

God, I know that You prefer to send mercy, not judgment. Let us hear Your heart and intercede for our cities, standing as oaks of righteousness to extend Your mercy. In Jesus's name, amen.

Eleven

Even Sodom

GOD DOES NOT hinder the healing of our land. Rather, our apathy and unbelief keep us from grasping the potential offered to us in the gospel of Christ. Do not marvel that entire cities can be saved. Scripture tells us that nations will come to our light and kings to the brightness of our rising (Isa. 60:1–3).

ALL WE LACK IS CHRISTLIKENESS

"Then He began to reproach the cities in which most of His miracles were done, because they did not repent" (Matt. 11:20). Jesus has a word to say, not only to us as individuals, but to entire cities as well. In anger He rebuked Chorazin, Bethsaida, and Capernaum (vv. 21, 23); with tears He cried out to Jerusalem (Luke 13:34). Yes, Jesus spoke to entire cities and expected them to repent, and He expects cities today to repent as well. The scale is different, but the grace to change is the same. Yes, Christ's message sounds a trumpet loud enough for whole cities to hear and be turned.

It was in this very context of reproving communities, however, that Jesus made a statement that unveiled God's redemptive power that is waiting and available for even the most wicked of cities. Listen to His rebuke and its hidden promise.

He said, "For if the miracles had occurred in Tyre and Sidon which occurred in you, they would have repented long ago in sackcloth and ashes" (Matt. 11:21).

Jesus said that His life, revealed in power, can bring even the vilest of cities—places that ought to be destroyed—to "sackcloth and ashes." The strategy, therefore, to win our cities is for the Church to reveal Christ's life in power. Yes, the revelation of Christ in us as individuals and the power of Christ displayed corporately through us as His body can turn our worst cities back toward God!

Today, many cities are ripe for revival. What hinders the turning of the people's hearts? The answer lies with the Church, with our sins of self-righteousness, apathy, and unbelief. The Lord said, "If My people humble themselves and pray, I will heal their land." (See 2 Chronicles 7:14.) Whether or not we actually attain Christ's level of faith, God "desires all men to be saved" (1 Tim. 2:4). With this in mind, Paul taught that entreaties and prayers should be made on behalf of all men, "for kings and all who are in authority" (1 Tim. 2:1–2). The sacrifice of Christ provides for the salvation of all men, and since the Father Himself desires all men to be saved, heaven waits only for the Church to act.

You may say, "But that was then. Our cities are worse now. They are beyond redemption." Not so. Jesus continued His rebuke of cities by saying, "If the miracles had occurred in Sodom which occurred in you, it would have remained to this day" (Matt. 11:23).

Amazingly, Jesus said even Sodom could find repentance!

I have heard many ministers compare Los Angeles or New York to Sodom. Fine. But these cities have seen hell, so now let the Church show them heaven. They need to see Jesus revealed in His Church. The promise of Christ is that even Sodom could repent in the atmosphere and revelation of Christ's power. If there is hope for Sodom, there is hope for your city as well.

THE OBSTRUCTION TO REVIVAL: COMPLACENCY

When we picture cities, we tend to see skylines and factories, streets and schools. Jesus, however, sees people. He beholds husbands arguing with wives while their children tremble in fear. He sees drugs being sold on playgrounds and teenagers having abortions. He suffers at the bedside of the hospitalized and the shut-ins. The heart of Christ grieves with the loneliness of the elderly and identifies with the struggle of the handicapped.

Yes, the eyes of the Lord see all things, but His heart probes the spirit and humanity of the city. From His eternal perspective He also beholds the most terrible event known to man. He sees the overwhelming horror, the utter despair an unsaved soul experiences as one realizes he is, indeed, dead and going to hell. And, in the midst of it all, He sees the Church—His Church, purchased at the cost of His own precious blood—sitting comfortably, remote control in hand, watching television.

Jesus does not have a problem with the hot or cold dimensions of life. It is the lukewarm that He will spew from His mouth (Rev. 3:15–16). What stopped the cities of Chorazin, Bethsaida, and Capernaum—communities that already had the blessing of Christ's healing—from embracing ongoing renewal? They assumed Christ's love was given only to enrich them. All they saw were the rewards of Christ without understanding His requirements.

The Church today is so similar in attitude to those ancient cities that it is frightening. The majority of the first-century saints gave their lives to Christ with the full knowledge that they would face persecution, suffering, and possibly death for their faith. Such was the character and vision of the Church in the first century.

The main emphasis of much of our Christianity, however, is to help believers become "normal." So much of our contemporary teaching keeps alive the very nature Jesus calls us to crucify. We need to reevaluate our preaching. Are we preaching the cross and the call to follow Jesus? What are we training our people to become? Please hear me; the Father's goal is not merely to bless us but to transform us into the image of His Son. He desires to use us to turn our families, communities, and churches back to Him. But God has made no provision for the healing of our land apart from the Church becoming Christlike. Once we realize this vital truth, we shall return to the holy source of New Testament Christianity, and our cities will have hope for redemption. When the Church demonstrates the love and power of Christ, repentance and revival can occur even in a place like Sodom.

KINGDOM-CONQUERING FAITH

Often I have heard Christians presumptuously state what they were "going to do to the devil." The outcome, however, has often been a testimony of what the devil did to them. At one time or another we have all fallen into boasting of our plans or achievements only to fall headlong, tripped by our own pride. Consequently, it is vital to recognize the pitfalls of presumptuous or arrogant "faith" before we approach our cities.

Nevertheless, while we want to avoid the excesses of presumption, the consequences of unbelief are worse. Jesus never rebuked anyone, saying, "O ye of too much faith." We have suffered because we have been too weak to believe God's promises. Regardless of excesses on either side of the faith issue, there *is* a legitimate dimension of faith that is coming from God. It is motivated by love and guided by wisdom, and it is coming from heaven to win the lost in our cities. It is no less powerful than the faith of those who "turned the world upside down" in the first century.

Abraham exercised this same faith in respect to the promise of God. Not wavering in unbelief, he grew strong in faith. He knew the heart of God and that it is the Lord's very nature to give "life to the dead" and call "into being that which does not exist" (Rom. 4:17). Abraham knew that if the Lord had but ten righteous men, He could deliver Sodom! God is giving us this kind of faith for our cities.

Look at the achievements of our forefathers in faith. Remember, these individuals served God in the Old Testament. God has given greater promises to us (Heb. 11:40). Through faith, God's people "conquered kingdoms, performed acts of righteousness, obtained promises, shut the mouths of lions, quenched the power of fire, escaped the edge of the sword, from weakness were made strong, became mighty in war, put foreign armies to flight" (Heb. 11:33–34).

Many Christians think knowing the promises is the same as obtaining them. True faith literally *obtains* the promises of God. In ancient times, through faith, men "conquered kingdoms." Faith can conquer our cities now! Faith can draw Christ's very righteousness into the Church, enabling us to lay down our lives for our neighborhoods as Jesus did for the world.

Our flesh says, "I am weak." Yes, but weakness is an improvement over all who are strong in their own strength. Through faith, which works through grace, we grow from "weakness," and in Christ we are "made strong." Faith "shut the mouths of lions"— those voices that would otherwise devour us with discouragement or fear. Because of Christ's accomplished victory, and through the knowledge of His Word, we are learning to become "mighty in war." We know that if evil can enter our cities through our negligence, evil can be driven out through our diligence. Indeed, it is possible to put the "foreign armies" of hell "to flight."

You might ask, "But does this fit into my eschatology?" Our "eschatologies" can be an excuse for unbelief. The fact is that we do not know when Jesus is returning. What we do know is that the devil is here now and has invaded our cities. Every generation has had to deal with the condition of their era, even those indicators that reinforce change and renewal are impossible.

Yet, where is the Church today? The body of Christ has been trapped in a doctrine that says that between now and when Jesus returns, only apostasy and more evil will exist. Paul warned about this time, saying, "In later times some will fall away from the faith" (1 Tim. 4:1). Knowledge and correct doctrines, as important as they are, should not be confused with actual faith. Jesus didn't say men would fall away from doctrines, but from faith. Matthew 15:21–28 tells of a Canaanite woman who approached Jesus, crying out for her daughter. She didn't know doctrinally that Jesus was the Son of God, and doctrinally, Jesus knew that His initial role was to only go to the "lost sheep of Israel." Yet, she had great faith, which Jesus also saw. Thus, He said, "O woman, your faith is great; be it done for you as you wish" (v. 28).

Each of us may have slightly different variations in peripheral doctrines, yet if we could unite in faith for our neighborhoods and cities, we might see great breakthroughs.

Paul said that in later times "some" will fall away. He did not say "all," but "some." From what will they fall away? They will fall away from *the faith*, not merely doctrines about faith! Faith believes that God is and that He is the rewarder of those who diligently seek Him (Heb. 11:6). If we believe in God, we must also believe He is the rewarder.

Let us become personal in this matter of the apostasy. At least for this next moment, let us not look for the apostasy anywhere else but in our own hearts. In matters of believing God to change us and our world, are we walking in *confident, expectant faith*? When we look at our cities, have we fallen away from the faith that believes God can, working through the Church, make a difference?

Apostasy is indeed here. However, those who see only a great falling away in the Church's future are, in their own way, in an offshoot state of unbelief. They may accurately know what God has done, but they have no faith for what He is doing. They are blind to the harvest, deaf to the outpouring of the Spirit, and ignorant of the emerging, unified Church. What should we do about such people? Pray for them with love and earnest zeal, for we too were unbelieving not long ago.

Yes, there is terrible darkness in the earth and a gross darkness upon the peoples; severe judgments are here, and they will get worse. However, the promise of God—no, the *command* of God—is full of both faith and power. In the midst of the most terrible of times, the greatest darkness, the Lord proclaims:

> Arise, shine; for your light has come, and the glory of the LORD has risen upon you. For behold, darkness will cover the earth, and deep darkness the peoples; but the LORD will rise upon you, and His glory will appear upon you. And nations will come to your light, and kings to the brightness of your rising.
>
> —ISAIAH 60:1–3

In the midst of the deepest darkness, God is sending the brightest light.

If we remain trapped in fear and unbelief, we are already a part of the "falling away from the faith." But if we are cleansing our hearts from sin, if we are uniting our hearts with that holy army being raised up in this hour, God will use us to bring nations to the light of the Lord. Kings will come to the knowledge of the Redeemer. Yes, there is hope even for Sodom to be turned back to God!

> *Dear Lord, we repent of our unbelief and apathy. Your grace saved us, and we know You can do anything. Give us faith—Your faith—for our cities. Help us see the expanse of Your love and its capacity to turn even Sodom back to You! In Jesus's name, amen.*

Twelve

The Wings of the Eagle

A NUMBER OF MY more prophetic friends do not see the United States featured or even surviving as a world power at the end of the age. In their view, there is no apparent reference to America in the Bible; thus they assume it will have suffered the consequences of accumulative sin. Some even see America as the modern manifestation of Mystery Babylon, mentioned in Revelation 17–18, and feel that God will at some time judge this nation's economy.

The prophetic images in Revelation and the daring defiance of God's ways seen in our legal system and culture add weight to their perceptions. Certainly, if there is no national repentance and return to God, we will align ourselves in attitude and practice with the nations judged by God in the past.

Yet, there are two Americas. One is indeed defiant and rebellious, constantly pushing the limits of morality. However, there is another America, a subset in society that does not make the news, nor does it embrace the wantonness of society. Within this group are tens of millions of believers, good people with sincere faith in Jesus Christ. These are those who are standing in the gap, who are like you, the reader, and who are salt and light to others.

Thus, because of the Christian seed in America, I do not see the United States being destroyed. However, I do see this nation facing severe chastening in the days ahead. The chastening will be deep and the blows mighty. America will break but then rise to its highest spiritual destiny. Whatever the conflict, its effect will help break the bonds of greed and immorality from the land.

When divine woundings come, remember God's hands also heal. Recall Jesus's statement to Peter, that Satan had demanded permission to sift Peter (and the disciples) like wheat. (See Luke 22:31.) There were "two Peters" fighting for dominance in the apostle's life: a superficial, ambitious chaff nature and a deeper "wheat" nature. America is much like Peter: strong, self-confident, and carnal. The Lord had to break Peter's self-will in order to unleash the spiritual side of the apostle.

Yet, it is possible that our prayers, our deepening godliness, and our fasting might cause conditions to change across the nation. With God all things are possible, so a way does exist within God's heart to avert the deep wounding altogether, but there are no guarantees.

THE REVELATION OF JESUS

As the Lord calls us to pray for the United States, I want to share with you my vision of God's plan for this nation. To do so, we will look into the Revelation of John. I know some think of America as a modern Babylon. To you I say that, even if we are exiled in Babylon, the command is still to pray for the nation, for in its welfare is our welfare (Jer. 29:7).

The last book of the Bible is, as its introductory sentence proclaims, the "Revelation of Jesus Christ." The book begins with John's profound encounter with the Lord Jesus in which the apostle collapses like a dead man. In chapters 2 and 3 we see Jesus correcting and encouraging His Church; in chapter 4 He is displayed as the King sitting upon His throne. In the next segment we behold the Lamb followed closely by His elect, where He opens the seals of judgment. And in the final section, Christ is revealed in a glory so expansive and brilliant that the earth and sky are swallowed in light, and in the holy city, the sun itself pales and is needed no more.

Throughout the book, Jesus is continually unveiled as the eternal commander of the heavenly host, leading a triumphant Church into His victory. If we do not see the revelation of the Son of God in this book, we will assume it is merely a prophecy of events. Without a vision of Christ, our fears magnify the judgments of God; we will miss the eternal champion who has written His autobiography before it happens.

It is with the reassuring knowledge of a conquering, invincible Christ that we step into the drama of End Time events. And, I believe, as we study the twelfth chapter of John's Revelation, we will see a prophetic picture of America's End Time role.

The chapter begins with a "great sign" appearing in heaven: "a woman clothed with the sun, and the moon under her feet, and on her head a crown of twelve stars" (v. 1). This woman is most often interpreted by Bible scholars as the true Church (although a few scholars see her as ancient Israel). Clearly, however, the early Christians did not recognize the woman as natural Israel since the Jews at that time were the leading persecutors of the Christians. I believe the Christians perceived this vision of a woman as a prophetic picture of themselves (Jews and Gentiles united as a new creation in Jesus Christ). Indeed, because her children hold the "testimony of Jesus," and since they overcome by the "blood of the Lamb," she is united to the Christian cause in nature and fulfills, in my opinion, the role of the "Jerusalem above," whom Paul says "is our mother" (Gal. 4:26; see also Heb. 12:18–23). She may also represent the deepest longings of all God's people from Abraham and the ancient Hebrews through the centuries into the New Testament era.

Verse 2 tells us that this woman is not aloof or quietly composed;

rather, she is "in pain to give birth," pregnant with the End Time promises of God. (See Galatians 4:19.) Her travail represents the most complete and focused intercession she can utter: the release of Christ in His many-membered body. In spite of Satan's attempts to abort or kill her child, she fulfills her holy mandate and gives birth to that which shall rule the nations.

Those few commentators who identify the woman as natural Israel logically identify her offspring as Jesus Himself. However, Matthew Henry, in his commentary on Revelation 12, writes that the woman is the Church. Of her offspring, he writes: "She was safely delivered of a man-child (v. 5), by which some understand Christ, others Constantine, but others, with greater propriety, a race of true believers, strong and united, resembling Christ, and designed, under him, to rule the nations with a rod of iron; that is, to judge the world by their doctrine and lives now, and as assessors with Christ at the great day."

THE GREAT EAGLE

As compelling and profound as the above interpretation is, my purpose is to identify for our intercession a scriptural understanding of God's purpose for America. After the woman gives birth, great conflict increases between the kingdom of God and Satan, first with a war in heaven, then with the dragon warring with the rest of the woman's offspring. Knowing his time is short, the devil rages against both the woman and her seed. But John tells us that, to protect her, "the two wings of the great eagle were given to the woman" (Rev. 12:14).

Commentators offer various interpretations as to who or what is represented by "the great eagle." *Jamieson, Fausset, and Brown's Commentary on the Whole Bible* states: "The great eagle is the world power...in early Church history, Rome, whose standard was the eagle, turned by God's providence from being hostile into a protector of the Christian Church. As 'wings' express remote parts of the earth, the two wings may here mean the east and west divisions of the Roman empire."

According to this 1871 commentary, early Christians interpreted the "great eagle" as the Roman Empire. In partial fulfillment of John's prophecy, under Constantine in 312, great protection did indeed come to the early Church. (Constantine himself was viewed as the "male child...caught up to God" through his vision of the cross, and he also "ruled the nations.")

This interpretation by the early Church, that a great nation would be turned to God to protect the Church from persecution, offers a legitimate faith pattern for us. Consider this: the symbol of the United States is, in fact, the great eagle! And while we may argue about the future, let us acknowledge the past: the wings of this eagle have indeed provided refuge for persecuted peoples for hundreds of years! *It is within the realm of faith-possibilities that the great eagle mentioned by John is a reference to God's plan to use the United States as a place of protection prior to the Rapture of the Church!*

SEEING AS GOD SEES

We cannot ignore the fact that there is great spiritual wickedness in high places over America. Still, as wickedness has become increasingly more brazen over the last thirty years, so the true Church in the United States has become purer, with maturing prayer and unity. Thus, we would be in great error to ignore the Father's intentions for America. This is not to limit His purpose with other nations around the world, either. Great evangelists will come from Africa and Asia; even Russia will have a mighty role in the End Time harvest. God's heart is for the nations. However, within the context of all that He is doing, we are confronted with a prophetic reference to the wings of the great eagle being given to the Church at the end of the age. Even bin Laden is credited with saying he desires to die in the belly of the eagle (in a terrorist act). Why should we not accept that the Almighty might have created the United States to protect Christians during the time of Satan's worst raging?

I realize that, for some, the mere suggestion that the United States may be the (or *a*) fulfillment of the "great eagle" resurrects all the negative impulses they have had about America. Some are convinced that America is the final manifestation of Babylon. Yes, the *spirit* of Babylon is here (as it is throughout the Western world), but this nation is *not* "Babylon" spoken of in Revelation 17 and 18. The "blood of prophets and of saints" (Rev. 18:24) has not been poured out upon America's streets. The exact opposite has been true: America has been a place of safety for the Church and a gift of divine protection for the nation of Israel!

Imperfect as this nation has been, still the United States has been a strong defense for the oppressed of the earth. Time and again the wings of this "great eagle" have been given to Christians fleeing persecution from around the world. Despite all the flaws, prejudices, and injustices committed by Americans, there simply has never been a nation whose spirit was *more* given to protecting the Church, or people in general, than the United States. Can any one nation on the earth better fit the prophetic profile of this verse?

BOTH WINGS

Revelation 12:14 states that "the two wings of the great eagle" were given to the woman (the Church). Why would John specify "the two wings," as though we did not know how eagles fly? I believe the Holy Spirit wants us to know God's will is not just sheltered under the eagle's "right wing." There are divine passions sheltered under the "left wing" as well. Christian Republicans ought to pray for and publicly support the interests of Christ as they are revealed in the Democratic Party: care for the poor, civil rights, and protection for the environment. Likewise, believing Democrats should cross the aisle and take strong pro-life stands and also publicly resist the legalization of perversion under the guise of freedom. I believe the Spirit of God has set His sights upon this nation. America has a unique role in End Time events that will take both wings to fulfill.

Will there be a wounding, a chastening of our land? If the prayer movement staggers, if we put down our spiritual vigilance, increased difficulties will be almost inevitable, especially if the entertainment industry continues to embrace the deep things of hell. However, I am fully convinced that whatever happens, it will be filtered by the mercy of God and redeemed to serve His purpose. I also believe that our Father will increasingly capture the soul of America until "the two wings of the great eagle" are given to the woman.

Lord, we want to see this nation as You see it. Forgive us for being critical. Forgive us also for blind patriotism. Lord, only You can turn this nation around, but we believe You can and will do it! Almighty God, empower us to this task, and grant that the wings of the great eagle might be given to Your Church. In Jesus's name, amen.

Part Three

The Anointing to Build

Our Father is the Creator. The Holy Spirit is the Helper. Jesus is the Word. If we will simply obey what Jesus says, the Holy Spirit will help us, and the Father will establish us as His living house.

Be strong and courageous and get to work.
Don't be frightened by the size of the
task, for the Lord my God is with you;
he will not forsake you. He will see to it
that everything is finished correctly.

1 Chronicles 28:20, TLB

Thirteen

The Apostolic Anointing

WORKING WITH THE Holy Spirit, citywide church leaders are receiving the Lord's concern for the entire living Church in their regions. To the degree they are building one body of Christ in their city, they are actually functioning under an apostolic anointing.

However, before we proceed further into this section, there are certain apprehensions I want to defuse. The first is that some may think our goal is to build a new denominational structure. This is completely untrue. The zeal that consumes us—as well as the love that compels us—is for our Father's house. Our goal, which we believe is God's goal, is to see the born-again Church functionally and relationally united under the blood of Christ.

It is our perception that the Lord does not want to eliminate denominational relationships or to separate congregations from the heritage of their forefathers. The Lord does not want to *eliminate*—but to *integrate*—what we each have received, that light may be given "to all who are in the house" (Matt. 5:15). We believe God's purpose is not to break off national affiliations but to heal and establish relationships locally.

We also want to remove any sense of human pressure concerning citywide prayer. The desire to pray with other pastors and congregations is a gift that God Himself works into the individual. To pluck this fruit prematurely is to have a crop that is both bitter and hard.

Those who embrace citywide prayer should do so because of revelation born of God. To seek to motivate pastors or leaders by pressure or manipulation will only breed resentment among them; they will fail to find the sweet pleasure that comes when leaders willingly seek God together. If you are concerned about your pastor, "pressure" heaven with prayer, and then leave this work of grace in the Creator's hands.

To those who are not yet involved, let me assure you: the nature of the born-again, praying Church is to appeal to God *for* you and others in the rest of the body of Christ. Anyone who exudes an attitude of superiority does not represent our heart or the heart of God. In truth, our focus is not on becoming leaders but on becoming followers of Jesus; not on a new doctrine but on obedience to the directives of Christ. We consider all elitism to be arrogant and an attitude God resists. The humbling of ourselves from religious pride was the first stronghold to fall, enabling us as pastors from different denominations to flow together. God help us that elitism not be the first sin to arise in this new stirring of God!

Our prayer is that this message will help initiate a new and holy beginning of the house of the Lord in your city. Let us also note that if a congregation recognizes Jesus as Lord and sees the need to be spiritually reborn—if they hold to the truth of the Scriptures and long for the personal return of the Lord Jesus—then we receive them as our brethren. We recognize that Jesus is not only the way to the Father, but He is also the bridge to one another. We present to you no other organization beyond cultivating the holy bond we each have with all who are born again in Christ.

What Is the Apostolic Anointing?

The first-century apostles left us more than their words; they also left us their anointing, through which we can build the house of the Lord. As we submit to their instructions, and as we are built upon Christ the cornerstone, grace is being granted to restore the living house of the Lord.

First, I am not suggesting each city select someone to be an apostle, nor am I implying that, in today's church, all who say they are apostles are, in fact, apostles. If I can speak honestly, I think calling oneself an apostle is counterproductive to uniting the body in the city. It implies that the other pastors and churches will, at some point, have to submit to you. Additionally, among the spectrum of pastors interested in praying, there are some who believe there were only the original twelve apostles, and there are others who actually know twelve people who call themselves apostles. The end result is that unity is broken. We really need to focus on Jesus, build unity through relationships and trust, and work to expand the unity, allowing love and humility to guide us.

However, just because we are not designating an individual as an apostle doesn't mean we are incapable of acting under an apostolic anointing. What is an "apostolic anointing"? In the same way a pastor is empowered by God to unselfishly care for his local congregation, so the apostolic anointing awakens local leaders to work together for the benefit of the expanded citywide body of Christ. It is a love-motivated awareness that the Church is one, and, as such, when one member suffers we all suffer.

Again, when I speak of an apostolic anointing, I am not necessarily referring to the office or restoration of modern apostles. I think if we want to honor a proven leader, one who has raised spiritual sons and daughters, who has, because of his virtue and balance, the respect and honor of other leaders in an area, perhaps we could identify him as a spiritual father. Such a term is more endearing (if it is true) than controversial.

However, whether God gives us apostles or not, we already have one who is our apostle: Christ, "the Apostle and High Priest of our confession" (Heb. 3:1). Although invisible, it is He who is guiding, building, and setting in order His Church. He is with us, even to the end of the age. When I speak of this anointing, I am referring to a unique grace coming from Christ the Apostle, through the first-century apostles, that is settling upon obedient leaders in local Christian fellowships today. These citywide pastors, leaders, and intercessors are reading the apostolic directives given to the early Church as though the New Testament was just written yesterday specifically for them:

> There is one body and one Spirit, just as also you were called in one hope of your calling; one Lord, one faith, one baptism, one God and Father of all who is over all and through all and in all.
>
> —EPHESIANS 4:4–6

MAINTAINING FREEDOM IN DIVERSITY

Those building together are not intimidated by the strengths of our leaders. Rather, they appreciate and respect the diversity of ministry in the citywide church. In our city, at various times, we have had leaders who had a unique grace to fight abortion issues; others had strong youth ministries; still others had wisdom to establish small groups. Why not learn from each other? We recognize that God has been at work, teaching and guiding leaders to serve in specific strengths and graces. We recognize that each individual pastor or ministry in the city is a unique product of the grace of God; we need one another to complete the work God has for our city.

Our uniting with other congregations and ministries must be free of subtle desires for control. There will be times when local pastors must face issues such as flagrant sin in a church leader or the difficulties of a church going through a split. These hurdles will be better solved by a team of leaders from the citywide church. If an individual is practicing obvious sin or teaching blatant heresy, he should be approached in meekness according to the Lord's instructions in Matthew 18:15–17. However, our focus is not upon where we have come from but upon where we are going and with whom. After love and friendship are established, correction, in many cases, will take care of itself.

Some in the past have tried to unite the Church through governmental structure. This is a hard task, for it immediately presents something other than Christ to rally around. Let's keep our focus upon the Lord. If you are building together, pastors must truly have faith in Jesus Christ; you must honor the Scriptures as the word of God. Our unity, though, is simply defined: we have each received the Lord Jesus Christ into our lives, and, because of Him, we are one now with each other. (See John 17.) The Lord Jesus Christ needs to be the living centerpiece of our unity. Let us maintain the standards we each have received from God without putting any burden upon one another other than genuine love.

"Now the Lord is the Spirit; and where the Spirit of the Lord is, there is liberty" (2 Cor. 3:17). I am listing liberty as a vital priority because our spiritual freedom is an evidence of the presence and involvement of the Lord.

"It was for freedom that Christ set us free; therefore keep standing firm and do not be subject again to a yoke of slavery" (Gal. 5:1). Without freedom to maintain differing doctrinal views or procedures on certain peripheral issues, we will only be exchanging an old form of religious slavery for a new one.

There will be great variety and power released as individuals with contrasting gifts begin to flow together. In Acts 13:1–2 we read of "prophets and teachers" who were "ministering to the Lord and fasting." Not out of corporate board meetings but out of corporate prayer and dependency upon the Lord came divine directives and ministry provisions for the Church: "The Holy Spirit said, 'Set apart for Me Barnabas and Saul'" (v. 2).

(It is important to note that the only time when we see the Holy Spirit commissioning apostles, outside of those who had been with Jesus, the event is birthed through citywide unity and prayer. Now, let me balance that statement by saying I know that, through the ages, God has raised up unique leaders who, with apostolic authority, founded denominations and international associations that changed the world around them. However, shouldn't we at least be mindful of the credibility and authority given the citywide church to recognize and ordain those whose life exemplifies the Christ-centered unity portrayed by leaders in the early Church?)

Let us also remember that the authority of the apostolic anointing is not merely an administration of church order; it is the administration of *Christ* in His Church, with all the esteem and diversity that emerges through a many-membered body. We need church administration, of course, but the "administration of Christ" is not to be confused with the ability to organize church dinners or special events. We all appreciate good administrators who streamline operations and facilitate the success of our projects, but the apostolic anointing draws our attention to the plan of God for our region.

APOSTOLIC PRAYER

At the core of the apostolic anointing is prayer. The early apostles were devoted to the words of Jesus and citywide prayer, meeting daily for prayer at 3:00 p.m. in the temple. These leaders were deeply dependent upon the power of God in their lives. The apostolic anointing is not something that simply falls on someone who always had a natural ability to lead; it falls upon those leaders who have come to the end of themselves, who are desperate for a true move of God in their cities and dependent upon God to produce it.

Apostolic prayer is concerned with the foundations of the Church being laid upon the work of Christ on the cross and the work of the cross in the believer. Indeed, apostolic prayer is also a "birthing prayer." Paul taught, "My children, with whom I am again in labor until Christ is formed in you" (Gal. 4:19). There are dimensions in the ministry of the Church that will not come forth until pastors and intercessors pray in the power of this apostolic birthing of the Church.

Those under this anointing will be so inflamed with a passion for redemption that the Lord will lead them into extended periods of fasting and prayer. As a result of this apostolic prayer, of Christ actually being "formed" in the Church, many cities will be brought to deep repentance. Indeed, under the apostolic grace there will be those upon whose "prayer shoulders" God places the burden for their cities. They will not sleep without praying for their communities, actually assuming a place of responsibility for the spiritual condition of the region. They will see a direct correlation between their personal prayer life and the advances or retreat of the enemy in their city.

One may question such spiritual responsibility. However, it is not unlike the ministry Martin Luther carried in Germany. He said, *"If I miss prayer one day, I feel it; if I fail to pray two days, the entire church feels it; should I not pray three days, all Germany suffers."*

Finally, it is under the apostolic anointing that true spiritual fathers are being restored to the Church. When we consider the apostolic, let us think of mature leaders who care for the condition of the Church, who seek to restore the Church to Christlikeness, and who will walk in prayer and love until the Father's house becomes a place not only of divine visitation but also of God's habitation on Earth.

Let's pray:

Lord God, it is our fervent desire to see Your house restored in unity, love, and power. Yet we acknowledge that no house we build is worthy or capable of receiving You. Nevertheless, You have promised to take humble, contrite people, who tremble when You speak, and make of them a house. Lord, grant us fathers who serve under the Apostle of the Church: Jesus Christ. Father, we yield to Your ability to make us a united dwelling where prayer and love transform our communities. Master, give us, even Your Church in our city, an apostolic anointing. In Jesus's name, amen.

Fourteen

The Stone That the Builders Rejected

THE GOAL OF God in this new anointing is to return the Church to the simplicity and purity of devotion to Christ. The correct foundation is not only what Jesus did in securing our salvation, but it is also what He commands us now as Lord. Once the foundation is properly laid within us, the house of the Lord can be built.

BECOMING WISE MASTER BUILDERS

Paul said, "As a *wise* master builder I laid a foundation" (1 Cor. 3:10, emphasis added). The eternal foundation of the Church is the Lord Jesus Christ; we rest and build upon Him. It is wisdom to build the Lord's house with only Jesus in mind, for He must be the central figure of every effort; He must abide as the living source of all our virtue.

Yet, there is a tendency to unconsciously avoid the teachings of Christ in favor of some other emphasis from the Scriptures. We make our favorite teaching the cornerstone of our congregation rather than Christ Himself. Inevitably we find ourselves attempting to make disciples in our image instead of His.

Jesus said, "The stone which the builders rejected, this became the chief corner stone" (Luke 20:17). We cannot separate what Jesus *says* from who Jesus *is*. Christ and His Word are one. To the degree that we fail to teach what Jesus taught, we are actually rejecting

Him as Lord and unconsciously redefining the dimensions of the cornerstone of the Church.

Listen to how the Lord associates Himself with His teachings. He said, "He who rejects Me, and does not receive My sayings, has one who judges him; the word I spoke is what will judge him at the last day" (John 12:48). He warned, "Whoever is ashamed of Me and My words, of him will the Son of Man be ashamed when He comes in His glory" (Luke 9:26). He exposes our hypocrisy, saying, "Why do you call Me 'Lord, Lord,' and do not do what I say?" (Luke 6:46).

You see, Christ and His Word are inseparable. Jesus was not a man who became the Word but the eternal Word who became a man. His very core nature is the Word of God. And to reject or ignore what He says is to reject or ignore who He is.

We cannot build the house of the Lord if we do not honor and build upon the full spectrum of Christ's teachings. Unless we are teaching our converts "all that [He] commanded," we are not making disciples (Matt. 28:19–20); we, in our church society, will always be trapped in spiritual infancy and religion.

Therefore let us honestly ask ourselves: In the building plan of our congregations, how much of an emphasis are we placing upon the words of Jesus? Is there a process in which new converts can become disciples of Christ?

If you are like most congregations, there is probably little focus given to systematic study and application of Christ's teaching. You see, if Jesus is truly the designer and builder of this house, then we must come to Him for the architectural plans. The building code of the kingdom must be obedience to the words of Christ.

> Therefore everyone who hears these words of Mine, and
> acts upon them, may be compared to a wise man, who built
> his house upon the rock. And the rain descended, and the

floods came, and the winds blew, and burst against that house; and yet it did not fall, for it had been founded upon the rock.

—MATTHEW 7:24–25

Beloved, there is a storm coming; even now the sky has darkened and the first drops are falling. If we will endure, we must be built upon the rock. Please hear me: *you cannot build your house in a storm.* It is through the Spirit and words of Christ that the house of the Lord is built. This is exactly what Jesus meant when He said, "I will build my church; and the gates of hell shall not prevail against it" (Matt. 16:18, KJV).

THE APOSTOLIC FOUNDATION

Multitudes of Christians today know what Jesus did, yet they remain stunted in their spiritual growth. Why? Without realizing it, we have made the teachings of Paul the "cornerstone" of the Church. The apostle's emphasis centered upon salvation, faithfully bringing us to Jesus. With great wisdom Paul presented God's plan of redemption in Christ. Paul's message revealed what Christ did, but Paul himself was built upon what Christ said. Paul did not become the *apostle* Paul apart from the words of Christ dwelling in him richly.

But it is Jesus, not Paul, who perfectly reveals the Father. Christ through His Spirit and His Word, like no one else in history, has the power to restructure our souls, conforming us inwardly in true accessibility to God.

Obviously, my dear friends, we are not in any way against the rest of the Bible. Each year I seek to read the Bible through, often reading on my knees. I love *all* of God's Word. Yet, one time I spent three years just reading and repeatedly studying the Gospels. I am convinced we, as the Church, have lost sight of Jesus in the blur of Christianity. He must be to us the very cornerstone and foundation of our lives. Indeed, it was upon this foundation of His Spirit and words that the Lord has built and empowered the ministry in my life.

It is not as though I am alone in my view: all the New Testament writers are in absolute agreement with my emphasis on Christ. Indeed, Paul writes in 1 Timothy 6:3–4, "This is the sort of thing you should teach and preach, and if anyone tries to teach some doctrinal novelty and does not follow sound teaching (which we base on our Lord Jesus Christ's own words and which leads to Christ-like living), then he is a conceited idiot!" (PHILLIPS).

When we seek to build upon a foundation other than Jesus, the results are everything but Jesus. Only Christ can create Christians. If we focus on our "doctrinal novelties," seeking to be just different enough to attract more people than the congregation down the street, we have missed the entire purpose of both the gospel and the ministry of Christ.

Paul based his teaching on "Christ's own words." Look at what John taught: "Watch yourselves, that you might not lose what we have accomplished, but that you may receive a full reward. Anyone who goes too far and does not abide in the teaching of Christ, does not have God" (2 John 8–9). The priority of this hour is for the Church to abide in the teachings and Spirit of the Lord Jesus. From this foundation the house of the Lord will be built.

We have had our pet doctrines and our own particular emphases. We have been like Peter speaking to Jesus on the Mount of Transfiguration: "Lord, it is good for us to be here; if You wish, I will make three tabernacles" (Matt. 17:4). We are so ready to offer a plan to God instead of simply hearing and obeying Jesus. I believe the Father Himself has had enough of our ideas and advice. In His love He is interrupting our programs with the same word with which He interrupted Peter: "This is My beloved Son, with whom I am well-pleased; listen to Him!" (v. 5).

Lord Jesus, forgive me for following winds of doctrine instead of picking up my cross and following You. Help me now to return with my whole heart to Your words. Lord, I desire to abide in You. I recommit my life to You that You alone would be the focal point of all Your people. In Jesus's name, amen.

By Wisdom the House Is Built

T HERE WAS A small city with few men in it and a great king came to it, surrounded it, and constructed large siegeworks against it. But there was found in it a poor wise man and he delivered the city by his wisdom" (Eccles. 9:14–15).

THE FEAR OF THE LORD

The wisdom of God can take even a poor man, train him in the ways of the Lord, and give him a strategy to deliver a city. Throughout the ages the Lord has had His judges, generals, and kings who delivered the nation of Israel. In more modern times God has had His men like Wesley, Martin Luther, and Jonathan Edwards, individuals who turned their nations toward heaven. The chaos of our cities is not greater than the chaos that covered the deep, formless, pre-creation void. God's wisdom brought creation to order, and His wisdom can bring the Church back to order as well.

The Lord desires for us to possess His wisdom. How do we find it? "The fear of the LORD is the beginning of wisdom, and the knowledge of the Holy One is understanding" (Prov. 9:10). What is "the fear of the Lord"? It is the human soul, having experienced the crucifixion of self and pride, now trembling in stark vulnerability before Almighty God. It is this living awareness: God sees and knows everything. This penetrating discovery marks the holy beginning of finding true wisdom.

However, this perception of the living God is not a terrible reality, for it liberates the mind from the cocoon of carnality, enabling the soul to escape into the Spirit. For all the dynamic gifts through which Jesus revealed the Father's power, His delight was in the fear of the Lord. (See Isaiah 11:1–3.) Yes, it is the awe-inspiring wonder of man living in fellowship, not with his religion, but with his God. In such a state the obedient man is invincible.

You see, the enemy does not fear the Church because the Church does not fear the Lord. As the fear of the Lord returns to us, the terror of the Lord will be upon our enemies. The fear of the Lord is our wisdom.

LET WISDOM GUIDE YOUR BUILDING

"By wisdom a house is built, and by understanding it is established; and by knowledge the rooms are filled with all precious and pleasant riches" (Prov. 24:3–4). The Lord's house is built by wisdom. It is established as we compassionately seek to understand the needs of our brethren. After it is built and established, then knowledge fills the rooms with riches.

You may be asking, "Where do I begin?" James tells us that if we lack wisdom, we can "ask of God" (James 1:5). Proverbs 4:7 tells us, "The beginning of wisdom is: Acquire wisdom." Wisdom is within the grasp of every man. Ask for wisdom, but seek the Lord, for with Him there is sound wisdom stored up for the upright.

Do not panic if wisdom seems far from you. Jesus Himself "kept increasing in wisdom" (Luke 2:52). Ultimately those who knew Him marveled, wondering, "What is this wisdom given to Him?" (Mark 6:2). Jesus grew in wisdom, and so also shall you.

GOD'S MANIFOLD WISDOM

It is the everlasting purpose of God that through the Church His "manifold wisdom" might be known "unto the principalities and powers in heavenly places" (Eph. 3:10, KJV). Yes, the Lord has instructed us concerning love. Truly He has apportioned to us an effectual measure of faith. Now He desires to give to His Church wisdom.

However, the above scripture speaks of the "manifold" wisdom of God. There are "many folds" to the wisdom of God. Moreover, there is a difference between knowledge and wisdom. We certainly will perish for a lack of knowledge (Hosea 4:6), but knowledge by itself tends to puff us up (1 Cor. 8:1–2). Wisdom knows what to speak and when to speak it. Knowledge, especially doctrinal knowledge, must be administered through wisdom. Presented by itself, even knowledge about unity can be divisive.

Oh, how the Church desperately needs men and women in whose mind dwells the wisdom of God, a people who are intimately obedient to the ways of God! We have tried zeal, human ingenuity, and ambitious programs, but to little avail. We have endured but not overcome as we had envisioned. Now it is time for those who lack wisdom to ask of God and receive liberally from Him the wisdom to build His house.

THE PROPER EMPHASIS OF DOCTRINES

There are doctrines without which we cannot be saved, and there are doctrines that are of lesser importance. "Jesus is Lord" is an unalterable doctrine. "Christ died for sinners" is another. "Jesus Himself is returning" is still another tenet that is essential to true Christian life.

But *when* Jesus returns, whether pretribulation, midtribulation or posttribulation, is of lesser importance. As Jesus said, "Be on the alert—for you do not know when the master of the house is coming, whether in the evening, at midnight, at cockcrowing, or in the morning" (Mark 13:35). It simply is not wisdom to argue and divide over when He will return, but rather to remain on the alert. Defining our doctrines is important. We need to clarify our belief systems so our perceptions of truth might be purposefully structured and overlaid correctly upon the Scriptures. Without such organization we have little hope of attaining the full benefits of our salvation. However, we can have all the right doctrines and still live outside the presence of God if our hearts are not right. Jesus said, "By this all men will know that you are My disciples, if you have love for one another" (John 13:35).

The outcome of right doctrines is love—love that covers other Christians and builds up the body of Christ; it forgives when offended and serves without hidden motives. It goes extra miles ungrudgingly. If our doctrines are not producing this kind of love, they are a smoke screen that will keep us separate and outside the house of the Lord. Let me give an example. In the first-century Church there was a controversy concerning eating meat sacrificed to idols. Paul had his views, while others had theirs. (See 1 Corinthians 8:8; Acts 15:29; Revelation 2:20.) But when he wrote on this subject, he said, "Now concerning things sacrificed to idols, we know that we all have knowledge. Knowledge makes arrogant, but love edifies" (1 Cor. 8:1).

Paul put love *above* knowledge. Everyone had a doctrine or conviction on the subject. In another epistle Paul prayed that the Ephesians would "know the love of Christ which surpasses all knowledge" (Eph. 3:19). The love of Christ "surpasses all knowledge." Even as Jesus bears with our ignorance because of love, so we must set our priorities according to His love and overlook that which will be more easily communicated as our relationships mature.

It is true that without knowledge we will perish, but knowledge without love is itself a state of perishing. To build the right foundation of the city church, therefore, we must all be in agreement about Jesus and His command to love one another. Greater wisdom than this will not be given concerning building the house of the Lord.

THE WISDOM FROM ABOVE

There are realistic steps toward seeing prayer and the house of the Lord established in your area. If wisdom shall build the house, it is important to define this dimension of Christ's nature. James 3:17 tells us the wisdom from above "is first pure." We cannot build the Lord's house with selfish or ambitious motives. Our desire should be to see the Lord satisfied. Therefore, our labors must be for Jesus, not self. It must be the love of Christ that compels us, not a desire to rise in prominence among men. Divine wisdom is next "peaceable" (v. 17). Peacemakers are sons of God; they are men and women of wisdom. Their wisdom lies in their understanding of the sublime and powerful ways of God. This wisdom is not born merely of intellectual study. Rather, because they have accepted the Lord's reproof, truth dwells in their innermost beings. The same eternal voice that brought correction "in the hidden part" is now rewarding them, granting them to "know wisdom" (Ps. 51:6).

The wisdom from above is also gentle and reasonable. We must be more willing to serve than to lead, more willing to be corrected than to teach. Where we see a need, such as in the areas of initiating prayer or administration, we should be given to fill the gap. But we must also be quick to surrender our task to any whom the Lord raises without feeling as though we have failed because another more qualified has arrived.

True wisdom is not stubborn but is willing to yield to other ministries and perspectives. It must be unyielding in regard to the deity and centrality of Christ and yet fully aware that God desires all men to be saved "with gentleness correcting those who are in opposition, if perhaps God may grant them repentance" (2 Tim. 2:25).

While the wisdom of God is meek, it is also "unwavering, without hypocrisy" (James 3:17). This is wisdom born out of vision, not organizational skills. It is unwavering because it sees that the builder of the house is Christ. It is genuine, "full of mercy and good fruits," overlooking mistakes, helping the weaker congregations, and disarming suspicion and fear with the credibility of Christ's unfailing love.

> *Dear Lord, You promised that if we lacked wisdom, You would give it to us liberally. We fear being trapped in our own ways with our own ideas. God grant us wisdom, plans, and strategies. Grant us the holy fear of Yourself, that You would become to us wisdom, knowledge, and strength. In Jesus's name, amen.*

Sixteen

The Dynamics of Revival

I N A MOVE of God some will be willing to die for what God is doing, and some outside it will be eager to kill them. Nevertheless a great harvest is coming, and it will emerge on a worldwide scale. When it comes, its underlying strength will be a passion for men's souls and the proclamation of a living word from God.

THE LORD'S WARNING

In every generation God has a harvest He seeks to reap through revival. Without fail, however, there will be those who stand in direct opposition to His purpose. In spite of persecution, the Lord sends His servants, fully knowing that "some of them they will kill and some they will persecute" (Luke 11:49). We will either receive the word God is speaking, or we will seek to kill it.

You may ask, "With so much falsehood, how do we know a true stirring of God's Spirit?" The answer is not as complex as it seems. Is the message a call to return to Jesus? Is it scriptural and being spoken by more than one voice? Is there a living witness in your own heart that what is spoken is true? Ultimately, the ability to discern whether a teaching is truly from God rests in our willingness to obey Him. Regarding His own teaching, Jesus said, "If any man is willing to do His will, he shall know the teaching, whether it is of God, or whether I speak from Myself" (John 7:17).

Assuming a message is genuinely from the Lord, there yet remain many risks. We will have to humble ourselves. There will be opportunities to stumble over the weaknesses of the Lord's servants, or, conversely, we will be tempted to overly exalt them. There will be suffering, and our motives will be tested. Through it all we will truly discover what is more important to us, the approval of men or the approval of God.

It is an awesome but fearful thing to be a church leader during a time when God is seeking a harvest. In truth, it is not only the harvest that is being weighed but also the very soul and character of those in leadership. In a move of God the gray routine of life ends. Both good and evil gravitate toward a state of fullness, stimulating prophets and "Pharisees" alike to their true natures.

BEWARE OF BECOMING AN "EXPERT"

Prior to the time of Christ's birth, the Pharisees were actually among the noblest men in Israel. As the cultural descendants of the Maccabees, they should have rejoiced in Christ's birth, but instead they ultimately were responsible for His death. By the time Jesus's ministry began, they were motivated not by their love of God but by their love of recognition and other personal ambitions. The Pharisees were not the only threat to the moving of God among the people; there were also the "lawyers." While our lawyers are experts in civil law, the lawyers of Jesus's day were recognized as experts in Mosaic Law. Because their livelihood was based upon the popularity of their explanations, it was very difficult for them to recant their errors. Instead of repenting, they compounded their doctrinal mistakes by defending them. Thus, they entered deeper into deception.

Like the Pharisees, the lawyers found their position in Jewish society threatened by the success of Jesus. It was not long before they were plotting with the Pharisees to stop Jesus, utilizing fear, slander, and physical violence against Him.

Jesus said, "Woe to you lawyers! For you have taken away the key of knowledge; you did not enter in yourselves, and those who were entering in you hindered" (Luke 11:52). The "key" to unlocking the power of knowledge is obedience. If we know spiritual things, we are blessed if we do them (John 13:17). But if we ourselves are not "entering in," we will find fault with those who are. More, we will attack those whom God is using. Thus, we cause to stumble those who would have otherwise entered. We become the modern "lawyers" who have "taken away the key of knowledge."

DYNAMICS OF REVIVAL

However, the major hindrance to revival is not the "Pharisees" and "lawyers." The main barrier is our own lack of love. It is to our shame that the devil desires men's souls more than the Church does. Therefore we must realize that revival will not sweep our land until we possess Christ's passion for the lost. Our authority must spring from a love of souls lest unity degrade into another wind of doctrine, again blowing us off course from true Christlikeness.

There are a number of essentials for revival. Here we will consider three of them: compassion, prayer, and the proclamation of an anointed word from God. Let us consider the first, Christ's compassion for the lost. God loves the world. We must look at our world in its sinfulness through the same mercy with which Christ gazes upon us. It requires no great insight to perceive the wickedness in our world. Clear vision rests in the heart of the pure: they see God, and, knowing His redemptive mercy, they reach out to the lost.

Indeed, one of our primary objectives in connecting congregations is that through our unity Jesus will be revealed. It is Christ's glorious presence in the Church, in contrast to the increasing darkness in our cities, that will draw multitudes to Him. Therefore, in all our labors to build the Church, we have in our view the "nations" that shall stream to the house of the Lord. (See Isaiah 2:2.)

The second essential to revival is prayer. You will remember that the early disciples had been in prayer prior to the outpouring of the Spirit. Afterward they continued in prayer, which released the Church into ongoing breakthroughs in God. The will of God is escorted to the earth through prayer. It is as simple as this: revival is an answer to prayer; if we do not pray, there will be no revival.

The third dynamic that actually lifts revival into a national or worldwide awakening is the proclamation of a living word from God. It is a message anointed with more than just insight or edification. It is truth declared in power that comes with signs following. The apostles' message came with such light that it broke demonic strongholds over the great span of cultures in the Middle East. In the major movings of the Holy Spirit, this anointed proclamation of God's Word has typically been a part of the substructure of revival. When John the Baptist stirred the nation of Israel, historians tell us that between seven hundred fifty thousand and one million people were baptized through his ministry. What was the origin of such an anointing? "The word of God came to John" (Luke 3:2). It was no mere "teaching" or "fresh insight" that motivated John, but a commission from God to herald His Word (John 1:6).

The nature of John's ministry was simple: He was "the voice of one crying in the wilderness" (Luke 3:4). The One crying in the wilderness was the Spirit of God; John was His voice. In preparation for Christ's coming, God Himself was changing the landscape of men's hearts—mountains were coming down; valleys were lifted up. God was doing something, saying something, and John carried the burden of God to the people.

On the Day of Pentecost three thousand souls were swept into the kingdom of God. On a natural level there was no mass evangelistic program. The fire of conviction fell under Peter's anointed word. His message was exactly what God was saying to the world: Jesus rose from the dead; He is the Christ! Thousands were pierced to the heart and immediately changed. God was launching the Church; Peter was God's voice.

The Lord has always used His Word to shepherd His people out of apostasy, progressively restoring them to the fundamentals of the faith. We should note that, since the Middle or Dark Ages, global awakenings have also brought the Church closer to the purity of New Testament order. Consequently, Martin Luther's proclamation that "the just shall live by faith" did more than win the nation of Germany; it restored truth to the Church. Wesley's message of his "salvation experience with the witness of the Holy Spirit" not only saved England from a revolution such as the French were experiencing, but it also brought the Church closer to the purity of the gospel.

The majority of the reformers not only kindled revival but also were used by God to restore *specific truths* to the body of Christ. As John the Baptist was the voice of one crying in the wilderness, so these men were the voice of God bringing truth back to the Church. The glory of the Lord had risen upon them, and nations came to their light. (See Isaiah 60:1–3.)

The message that brings worldwide awakening is that which embodies what God is doing and proclaims what God is saying. The revivalists brought not only souls to Christ but also the next phase in God's progressive renewal and restoration of the Church. None of those who impacted nations presented new or extra-biblical revelation; they brought anointed, *scriptural* truth to their generations.

Even today God's truth continues "marching on." What is the Lord doing today? It is obvious that, while the Holy Spirit is reaching the nations, He is also dissolving walls between congregations. The writings of contemporary Christian authors from many perspectives have been homogenized into our spiritual diet. In general, Christians today are less and less the product of one denomination. Additionally, different church affiliations have found themselves standing side by side fighting common enemies such as abortion, pornography, and the occult.

Where is all this going? A wonderful dawn is breaking upon the Church. While we have grown under the same teachers and fought against the same enemies, to our amazement we are discovering, in different ways, that the Lord has been guiding us all to Himself. This, we believe, is the anointed truth that God is speaking: It is time for the house of the Lord to be built. As Jesus steps forth from His house, I believe revival will break forth in many cities.

Our Strategy From God

While the harvest field of this coming revival is worldwide, we recognize that the specific battlegrounds are cities. In the Book of Revelation Jesus dealt individually with congregations in certain cities. Each congregation had a unique struggle as well as unique promises. You will also remember that the Israelites conquered the Promised Land city by city. Therefore, for us to touch a nation, we must focus upon its cities.

We are called to serve as a witness to confirm and help establish the praying, Christ-centered Church. We have seen that a divided city church cannot win the war for its city. And we know that corporate prayer is always the prerequisite for revival. Therefore, a citywide visitation of Christ is impossible until at least some measure of that city's congregations is committed to pray for revival.

Although many congregations will continue to be blessed of God independently of the citywide anointing, to impact the heavenly places and win the war for our regions we must be united in prayer. The spiritual void in the heavenlies, which gave room to the powers of darkness in the first place, must be filled by the alignment of the church on Earth with Christ in heaven. God's focus is uniquely upon this ripening, praying Church. Without any doubt, from the house of the Lord revival will burst upon our land.

Heavenly Father, grant us Your vision for revival! Open our eyes to Your strategies and wisdom, Your love and compassion. Help us not to be caught fighting what You are doing. We give ourselves to serving You in the simplicity of devotion to Christ. We commit ourselves to build Your house. In Jesus's name, amen.

Seventeen

Spiritual Authority and the Things We Love

WHILE THE DOCTRINES of Christianity can be taught, Christlikeness can only be inspired. By their humble and holy lives, this next generation of leaders will inspire multitudes. They will truly walk in Christ's love; they will be granted great authority.

The Church has many administrators but few examples of Christ; many who can explain the doctrines of Christianity but few who walk as Jesus walked. Indeed, while many stand in leadership today, not many function in the higher realms of authority that Christ purchased for His Church. However, a new badge of authority is coming to the Church. It will bring deliverance on a scale unprecedented; in some cases, entire cities will be turned toward God.

What is spiritual authority? It is nothing less than God Himself confirming with power the word of His servant. Moses exemplified spiritual authority when he warned unrepentant Pharaoh. The Spirit of God confirmed Moses's judgments with power that broke the pride of Egypt. Jesus manifested spiritual authority when He confronted demons in people, silenced storms, healed diseases, and then fulfilled redemption in resurrection power. The Father let none of Christ's words go unfulfilled.

The Bible provides us with many examples of those with spiritual authority. Every example tells us the same underlying principle:

those who are raised up by God are backed up by God. They will "decree a thing, and it will be established" (Job 22:28). Such is the nature of spiritual authority.

THE SOURCE OF AUTHORITY

Obviously, as pastors, leaders, and intercessors, we need to operate in greater authority. Yet while we enjoy a variety of graces that add to our personal edification, God gives us authority for one specific purpose: to fulfill His purposes on the earth. What are God's purposes? One main unveiling of the divine purpose is seen in the Great Commission. Jesus said, "All authority has been given to Me in heaven and on earth. Go therefore and make disciples of all the nations" (Matt. 28:18–19).

Christ gave the Church authority to make disciples. We have been much more successful in making converts than disciples. In our day, many are believers in Jesus, but few are truly followers of Christ. If the goal is discipleship, how do we accomplish this? We are to take our converts and teach "them to observe all that [Jesus] commanded" (v. 20). When the Church returns to teaching all that Jesus taught, our disciples will have authority to do all that Jesus did.

Yet, spiritual authority is not something we possess merely because we strive for it. We cannot buy it as Simon the magician attempted to do (Acts 8:18). The power of authority will not function simply because we copy the methods of another, as the sons of Sceva realized (Acts 19:14–16). Nor can it be attained automatically because we read books about building the Church. We cannot pretend to have spiritual authority. As we focus upon obeying the words of Christ, there are divinely ordained ways for Christ's authority to unfold in our lives.

From the beginning of our salvation we have enjoyed the Father's unconditional love. As we mature, however, there comes a time when the Father's love toward us seems conditional. As it was for Christ, so it is for those who follow Him. He said:

> For this reason the Father loves Me, because I lay down
> My life.
>
> —JOHN 10:17

Jesus lived in the deepest intimacies of the Father's love because He laid down His life for the sheep. If we will grow in true authority, we will do so by laying down our lives for His sheep.

Have you felt the drawing, the divine working of the Father bringing you into Christlike surrender? Be encouraged: He is equipping you for this next outpouring of His Spirit. But also be advised: your authority will be an outgrowth of your life laid down in love.

As leaders, we do indeed have *administrative* authority due to our positions in church government; however, *spiritual* authority transcends administrative authority. Here is the path to true spiritual authority: in full possession of our souls, without fear or intimidation by any outside source, we choose to lay down our lives for Christ's sheep. Yes, in full freedom, with avenues of escape plainly within view, we fearlessly surrender our souls to God. No one controls us but God, yet our lives are laid down, like Christ's, for the sins of men. When we could easily fight and win, yet turn the other cheek; when we are unjustly opposed, yet quietly endure—at those moments spiritual authority is entering our lives.

> No one has taken [My life] away from Me, but I lay it
> down on My own initiative.
>
> —JOHN 10:18

Jesus was not forced to accept crucifixion; He chose crucifixion. Christ's Gethsemane prayer was not an entreaty to escape the cross, for while Jesus was still in the garden, He told Peter, "Do you think that I cannot appeal to My Father, and He will at once put at My disposal more than twelve legions of angels?" (Matt. 26:53). Jesus had a choice: legions of warring angels and immediate personal deliverance, or death on the cross and deliverance for the world. He chose to die for us. The willful decision to lay down our lives as Jesus did is the very path upon which true authority develops. Jesus said, "I have authority to lay [My life] down" (John 10:18). His authority came in the laying down of His life. Our authority comes from the same source: picking up our cross and laying down our lives for others.

AUTHORITY, NOT CONTROL

Spiritual authority is the provision of God to transform the temporal with the power of the eternal. It is not something our flesh can imitate, nor is it found in the tone of our words or the gaze of our eyes. Divine authority requires divine sanction. This sanction comes from passing the tests of love.

When authority is administered without love, it degenerates into control. God does not call us to control His people but to inspire and guard them. The outcome of control is oppression, witchcraft, and strife. But the result of love is liberty and the power to build up and protect God's people.

True spiritual authority exists above the realm of fleshly control. Our lives, and the lives of those who follow us, are laid down on our own initiative. It is a choice we make because of love. Since true authority itself is born in freedom, freedom is what it breeds.

We will walk in either the true authority of love, the false authority of control, or no authority at all. Both false authority and no authority are rooted in fear, and we react to fear in either of two ways. The first reaction, which produces false authority, is to seek to control those around us, thus making the circumstances around us more predictable and less threatening. The other response to fear is to refuse to accept and exercise any authority at all. Many relationships are simply the pairing of these symbiotic needs: the desire to control and the willingness to be controlled. Both are fueled by overreactions to fear.

Scripture tells us, however, "There is no fear in love; but perfect love casts out fear" (1 John 4:18). Since true authority is built upon love, its goal is to liberate, not dominate. Therefore, before one can truly move in spiritual authority, he must be delivered from fear and its desire to control; he must be rooted and grounded in love.

AUTHORITY TO INSPIRE CHRISTLIKENESS

When our teaching about God and our obedience to Him are one, spiritual authority accompanies our lives. Jesus astounded the multitudes, for He spoke "as one having authority" (Matt. 7:28–29). What He taught was consistent with how He lived. Therefore, we also must live and display the virtue we seek to teach.

Dear pastor, if we seek to train our congregations to pray, we ourselves must first be intercessors. You may say, "But out of a congregation of several hundred, only three people join me for prayer." Then with those three develop your intercessor base. Do not be discouraged, for you will win others. But the measure of our success is not the numbers in attendance on Sunday mornings. God has given us people so we may train them, not merely count them. Of this group, those whom we inspire to live like Christ are actually the measure of our success, the test of our effectiveness in the ministry.

Another may say, "But I've never been a leader." When anyone lays down his or her life in Christ's love, others will see and follow. Whether you are a business owner, a housewife, or a teen, such a one can speak with confidence and authority as Christ's disciple.

In truth, if you are following Christ, others are following you. You are, indeed, a leader.

This next generation will not just teach the people; they will inspire the body of Christ to live like Jesus. Their example in all things will awaken godliness in those around them. From true virtue shall the leaders of tomorrow draw true authority, for when the nature of Christ is revealed, the authority of Christ soon follows.

AUTHORITY BORN FROM LOVE

As wide as our sphere of love, to that extent we have spiritual authority. We see this in the mother who loves her child. Such a woman has authority to protect, train, and nurture her offspring. *She has authority to protect what she loves.* The same is true of the husband over his family. His authority is not merely to rule but to establish his home in the life of Christ. True spiritual authority is born of love.

The individuals who love their local congregation have authority to build up that congregation. Their authority is not extended, however, beyond the boundaries of their love. If we love the entire body of Christ in a locale, our authority touches the lives of those in our city or region, either through the burden of prayer or through teaching or service.

The testing ground of all spiritual things is love, for love alone purifies our motives and delivers us from the deceitfulness of self. Even authority in spiritual warfare must be rooted in love. David gained the skills to slay Goliath, not on a battlefield, but by defending his father's sheep from vicious predators. He loved the sheep so much that he would even risk his life for them. So also we grow in authority as we protect our Father's sheep, the flock He has given us to love.

Authority is muscle in the arm of love. The more one loves, the more authority is granted to him. If we love our cities and are willing to lay down our lives for them, God will enlarge our hearts, granting us authority to confront principalities and powers.

However, no man should ever engage in confrontational warfare who does not love what he has been called to protect. If you do not love your city, do not pray against the ruling forces of darkness. Satan knows the genuineness of our love by the brightness of the glory that surrounds us. A man without Christlike love will soon shrink back and fail in spiritual warfare.

Therefore, in His mercy God restrains most Christians from understanding the doctrines of authority in spiritual warfare. For there are many things He has to say that we are not able to hear until the base of our love is expanded. In His love He protects us from presumptuously attacking the strongholds of hell and suffering loss. Yet, if we are truly anointed in God's love, the price to see our cities saved is not too great, for it is the price love always pays: the willingness to die for what we care for.

AUTHORITY TO BUILD UP THE BODY OF CHRIST

"For even if I should boast somewhat further about our authority, which the Lord gave for building you up and not for destroying you…" (2 Cor. 10:8). Many so-called "prophets" today think they are called, like Jeremiah, to "pluck up and to break down, to destroy and to overthrow" (Jer. 1:10). Jeremiah's message was to a people who were destined to be carried off into Babylon. He spoke to a people who did not have the Holy Spirit and the blood of Jesus, a nation that God Himself said was destined for captivity. (See Jeremiah 12:7.)

The whole commission of Jeremiah, though, was more than confronting sin. It also included promises of restoration and deliverance, "to build and to plant" (Jer. 1:10). To represent the heart of the Lord, which is the true prophetic role, the servant of God must know if the Holy Spirit is preparing to destroy or seeking to rebuild.

Today we are a people coming out of captivity, a people whom God is encouraging to build, as they did in the days of Nehemiah, Ezra, Haggai, and Zechariah. We have been in exile from the promises of God, but we are returning to rebuild the Lord's house. It is not a time to tear down the body of Christ; it is time to establish and to build up.

The authority coming to the Church in this next outpouring will be an authority to restore the local, citywide church. Like Paul's authority, ours will be given for building and encouraging and not for destroying.

God has this new leadership constantly before His eyes. Pastors from many denominations, along with their congregations, are meeting together in prayer, seeking to draw the very fire and heart of God into their souls. Emerging from this foundation of humility and prayer is a new authority to make disciples of Christ. Because their love encompasses the entire city, their authority reaches even into the heavenly places. They are beginning to impact the spiritual atmosphere of their cities; in many cases, they are becoming effective against the principalities and powers ruling there. These are the leaders whom God is raising up, whom He will back up with His power.

> *Dear Lord, make me a willing sacrifice. I desire Your authority, Lord. Give me courage to surrender in obedience, even when I do not see the outcome and when all I see is loss. Help me to trust as I walk through the narrow gate. Establish in me Your love that I might defend Your people with authority. In Jesus's name, amen.*

Eighteen

The House of Glory

T HE DEDICATION OF Solomon's temple offers us a picture of what God is seeking in the Church. The temple was built, and in great pageantry and celebration, it was consecrated to the Lord. Solomon offered a sacrifice of 22,000 oxen and 120,000 sheep. Then, immediately after the king prayed, for the first time in over four hundred years, the glory of God was manifested in full view of the people. We read, "Fire came down from heaven and consumed the burnt offering and the sacrifices; and the glory of the LORD filled the house" (2 Chron. 7:1).

If the Lord would honor the dedication of the physical temple with a visible manifestation of His glory, how much more does He seek to reveal His glorious presence in His living temple, the Church?

But there were prerequisites that occurred prior to this appearance of the Lord. First, it was not until Solomon's temple was actually built, with all its separate aspects connected together and covered in gold, that the glory of the Lord appeared.

Likewise, we also must be built together and "perfected in unity" if we would see the fullness of the Lord displayed among us and the world believe in Christ (John 17:23). There is no other aspect of life more glorious or wonderful than this.

The next requirement deals with our worship. The Lord was not revealed until the singers, trumpeters, and priests lifted their voices in praise and worship to God. We cannot overstate the need to be worshipers of God. Even now, in a number of church worship services, a faint, luminous glory is appearing, like a living cloud, drawn by the purity of the ascending worship.

However, there was another dimension of preparation that also preceded the revelation of glory. This prerequisite had to do with those in leadership.

> And when the priests came forth from the holy place (for all the priests who were present had sanctified themselves, without regard to divisions)…then the house, the house of the LORD, was filled with a cloud, so that the priests could not stand to minister because of the cloud, for the glory of the LORD filled the house of God.
> —2 CHRONICLES 5:11–14

Their divisions in the priesthood had been ordained by God according to individual families and unique purposes. These were not carnal divisions, born of jealousy or strife, but divisions of purpose, function, and timing. Yet, when the priests entered the holy place, God required they "sanctified themselves, without regard to divisions" (v. 11). In other words, when it came to building the temple and entering the holy place, the priests had to lower the priority of individual service, which in a sense divided them, and raise the priority of seeking God's glory, which united them. It was here, when they were "without…divisions," that the glory of God manifested.

So also today, God has appointed congregations in each city with different functions, graces, and talents, all of which are needed to meet the needs of a diverse surrounding culture. These differences, however, are not meant to divide us but to complete us. But if we desire to see the glory of God return to the Church, the divisions of purpose must be subordinate to the unity of Spirit.

Today, in meetings, conferences, and prayer groups, in one-on-one visits over coffee, and in church altars and citywide outreaches, increasing numbers of Christians are returning to Christ "without regard to divisions." Indeed, over the decades, tens of thousands of God-hungry pastors are surrendering afresh to the Lord in acts of holy consecration; they are seeking the glory of God. The outcome? The Church is being "fitted together . . . growing into a holy temple in the Lord; in whom [we] also are being built together into a dwelling of God in the Spirit" (Eph. 2:21–22).

Notice these words: "fitted together . . . built together." The true house of the Lord is revealed when the Church, "without regard to divisions," is "fitted together." Only then can the Church truly be unveiled as the temple of the Lord, "a dwelling of God in the Spirit."

The Source of Glory

> And the glory which Thou hast given Me I have given to them; that they may be one, just as We are one; I in them, and Thou in Me, that they may be perfected in unity [into a unit].
>
> —John 17:22–23

Jesus is not coming to give us a new form of church government or new doctrines and programs. He is coming to be glorified in His saints and marveled at by all who have believed (2 Thess. 1:10)! It was for this that He called us, that we may gain His glory (2 Thess. 2:14)!

Let us each see that God is building something in this hour that will far exceed our current definition of the Church. God is building us together into "a holy temple in the Lord," a place where His very glory shall be revealed!

Consider the words of the following prayer. It is our response to the Lord's call to build His house. God is calling us, not to lose our individual distinctions and callings, but to build something that fits us together, enabling us to build without regard to divisions.

If you see the vision of the house of the Lord, please pray with us...

> *Lord Jesus, I thank You for granting me a new opportunity to serve You. I repent of the areas in my heart where I allowed division and self-interest to guide my actions. Jesus, I want to see Your glory, even to abide as did Moses, in Your sacred presence. Master, I consecrate my heart, without regard to divisions, to Your sacred service. Before You I sanctify my life and my congregation to build the house of the Lord in my city. Amen.*

Part Four

Our Strategy:
Obedience to Christ

When Israel was united in its obedience to the Lord, it did not matter how many or how strong their enemies were; they were invincible in war. God fought for them. When the Church is obedient to Christ, God will fight for us as well.

Hear, O Israel, you are approaching the battle against your enemies today. Do not be fainthearted. Do not be afraid, or panic, or tremble before them, for the LORD your God is the one who goes with you, to fight for you against your enemies, to save you.

DEUTERONOMY 20:3–4

Nineteen

Exposing the Accuser of the Brethren

M ORE CONGREGATIONS HAVE been destroyed by the accuser of the brethren and its faultfinding than by either immorality or misuse of church funds. So prevalent is this influence in our society that, among many, faultfinding has been elevated to the status of a "ministry." The Lord has promised, however, that in His house accusing one another will be replaced with prayer, and faultfinding will be replaced with a love that covers a multitude of sins.

FIRST, A DISCLAIMER

This chapter is written specifically to expose the activity of the accuser of the brethren among born-again Christians. We will talk about faultfinding and slander extensively, but first let us acknowledge that there is more to this subject than can be said here. I have another book on discernment that goes much deeper into this theme. It deals with issues related to obvious sin, blatant heresy, cults, and aberrant behavior in churches and leaders. We also discuss issues concerning ministerial accountability, which in establishing would eliminate much warfare concerning speculative judgment and exaggerated faultfinding. Please check our Web site for this material.

For those concerned readers, please understand I am not suggesting we abandon discernment or position ourselves in some ethereal realm where everything is beautiful and true. No. We need to judge righteously. But there is a difference between righteous judgment and simply finding fault and judging after the flesh. The latter is what we are discussing here.

SATAN WANTS TO STOP YOUR GROWTH

In an attempt to hinder if not altogether halt the next move of God, Satan has sent forth an army of faultfinding demons against the Church. The purpose of this assault is to entice the body of Christ away from the perfections of Jesus and onto the imperfections of one another.

The faultfinder spirit's assignment is to assault relationships on all levels. It attacks families, congregations, and interchurch associations, seeking to bring irreparable schisms into our unity. Masquerading as discernment, this spirit will slip into our opinions of other people, leaving us critical and judgmental. Consequently, we all need to evaluate our attitude toward others. If our thoughts are other than "faith working through love," we need to be aware that we may be under spiritual attack.

The faultfinder demon will incite individuals to spend days and even weeks unearthing old faults or sins in their minister or congregation. The people who are held captive by this deceitful spirit become "crusaders," irreconcilable enemies of their former assemblies. In most cases the things they deem wrong or lacking are the very areas in which the Lord seeks to position them for intercession. What might otherwise be an opportunity for spiritual growth and meeting a need becomes an occasion of stumbling and withdrawal. In truth, their criticisms are a smoke screen for a prayerless heart and an unwillingness to serve.

That someone should discover the imperfections of their pastor or congregation is by no means a sign of spirituality. Indeed, we were able to see errors in the church *before* we were Christians! What we do with what we see, however, is the measure of Christlike maturity. Remember, when Jesus saw the condition of mankind, He "emptied Himself, taking the form of a bond-servant....He humbled Himself by becoming obedient to the point of death, even death on a cross" (Phil. 2:7–8). He died to take away sins; He did not just judge them.

No One Is Exempt

It is of some consolation that Christ Himself could not satisfy the "standards" of this critical spirit when it spoke through the Pharisees. No matter what Jesus did, the Pharisees found fault with Him.

If you personally have not consulted with and listened to the individual of whom you are critical, how can you be sure that you are not fulfilling the role of the accuser of the brethren? Even the "Law does not judge a man, unless it first hears from him" (John 7:51).

The enemy's purpose in this assault is to discredit the minister so it can discredit his message. I have personally listened to scores of pastors from many denominational backgrounds, and I have found that the timing of this spirit's attack upon their congregations was almost always just prior to or immediately after a significant breakthrough. The unchallenged assault of this demon *always* stopped the forward progress of their congregation.

When this spirit infiltrates an individual's mind, its accusations come with such venom and intimidation that even those who should know better are bewildered and then seduced by its influence. Nearly all involved take their eyes off Jesus and focus upon "issues," ignoring during the contention that Jesus is actually praying for His body to become one. Beguiled by this demon, accusations and counteraccusations rifle through the soul of the congregation, stimulating suspicion and fear among the people. Devastation wracks the targeted congregation, while discouragement blankets and seeks to destroy the pastor and his family or other servants of God in that local body of believers.

Nearly every believer reading this has faced the assault of the faultfinder spirit at one time or another. Each has known the depression of trying to track down this accusing spirit as it whispers its gossip through the local church: trusted friends seem distant, established relationships are shaken, and the vision of the congregation is in a quagmire of strife and inaction.

This enemy is not limited to attacks on local congregations, however. Its attacks are also citywide and national. Major publishers have made millions of dollars selling defaming books that are hardly more credible than gossip columns in the tabloids. Yes, in some situations there were ministers involved with serious sin, for which there are grave consequences. Correction for such iniquity, especially in a leader, should be administered according to the Word of God and, if need be, civil authorities. However, for most issues there are biblical ways to bring correction, ways that lead to healing and not to destruction. There are denominational supervisors as well as local ministerial associations who can review disputes privately. Instead, church leaders boldly challenge other leaders over issues that could be remedied privately in humility. Who hasn't become aware of the books, e-mails, and Web sites devoted strictly to criticizing other Christians? Lies and half-truths from such sources, unfortunately, circulate like poison through the bloodstream of the body of Christ—and how the Savior's Church gluttonously eats it up!

To mask the diabolical nature of its activity, the faultfinder spirit will often garb its criticisms in religious clothing. Under the pretense of protecting sheep from a "gnat-sized" error in doctrine, it forces the flock to swallow a "camel-sized" error of loveless correction. (See Matthew 23:24.) The methods used by those to "correct" violations of Scripture are themselves a violation of Scripture! Where is the "spirit of gentleness" of which Paul speaks in Galatians 6:1, the humility in "looking to yourselves, lest you too be tempted"? Where is the love motive to "restore such a one"?

In most cases, the person supposedly in error has never even been contacted before his alleged mistakes enter the rumor mill of the cities' congregations or media outlets. Only then, after the slander has been made public through a book, CD, or broadcast, does he become aware of his alleged faults. Brethren, the spirit behind such accusations must be discerned, for its motive is not to restore and heal but to destroy.

THE PURE EXAMPLE

The Church needs correction, and ministers and public leaders need accountability, but the ministry of reproof must be patterned after Christ and not the accuser of the brethren. When Jesus corrected the churches in Asia (Rev. 2–3), He sandwiched His rebuke between praise and promises. He reassured the congregations that the voice about to expose their sin was the very voice that inspired their virtue. After encouraging them, He then brought correction.

Even when a congregation was steeped in error, as was the case with two of the seven churches, Christ still offered grace for change. How patient was Jesus? He even gave "Jezebel…time to repent" (Rev. 2:20–21). After He admonished a congregation, His last words were not condemnation but promises.

Is this not His way with each of us? Even in the most serious corrections, the voice of Jesus is always the embodiment of "grace and truth" (John 1:14). Jesus said of the sheep, "They know his voice. And a stranger they simply will not follow, but will flee from him" (John 10:4–5). Remember, if the word of rebuke or correction does not offer grace for restoration, it is not the voice of your Shepherd. If you are one of Christ's sheep, you will flee from it.

THE ENEMY'S WEAPONS

To find an indictment against the Church, it is important to note the enemy must draw his accusations from hell. If we have repented of our sins, no record of them or of our mistakes exists in heaven. As it is written, "Who will bring a charge against God's elect? God is the one who justifies" (Rom. 8:33). And, "Their sins and their lawless deeds I will remember no more" (Heb. 10:17). In truth, Christ has "forgiven us all our transgressions, having canceled out the certificate of debt consisting of decrees against us and which was hostile to us; and He has taken it out of the way, having nailed it to the cross" (Col. 2:13–14).

Jesus is not condemning us, but He is at the Father's right hand interceding on our behalf. It is the devil who takes our sins and holds them before us. Let us, therefore, expose the weapons of the faultfinder spirit. The weapon used is accusation against us for our unrepented sins. Our failure to repent when the Holy Spirit desires to correct us opens the door for the accuser to condemn us. The voice of the enemy, however, never offers hope or extends grace for repentance. It acts as though it is the voice of God and we are guilty of the "unpardonable sin." The way to defeat the enemy in this arena is to disarm him by sincerely repenting of the sin, looking again to the atonement of Christ as the sum of all our righteousness.

Yet Satan seeks not only to accuse us as individuals but to blend into our minds criticisms and condemnation against others as well. Instead of praying for one another, we react in the flesh against offenses. Our un-Christlike responses are then easily manipulated by the faultfinder spirit.

Therefore, we cast down the accuser of the brethren by learning to pray *for* one another instead of preying *on* one another. We must learn to forgive in the same manner as Christ has forgiven us. If one has repented of his sins, we must exercise the same attitude of "divine forgetfulness" that exists in heaven. We defeat the fault-finder when we emulate the nature of Jesus: as a lamb, Christ died for sinners; as a priest, He intercedes.

The second weapon this demon uses against us is our past mistakes and poor decisions. Each of us has an inherent propensity toward ignorance. One does not have to read far into the history of the saints to discover they were not called because of their intrinsic wisdom. In truth, we all have made mistakes. Hopefully we have at least learned from them and developed humility because of them. This faultfinding demon, however, takes our past mistakes and parades them before our memory, criticizing our efforts to do God's will. His goal is to keep us in bondage to the past.

When the enemy pits us against one another, it first provokes us to jealousy or fear. The security of our place in life seems threatened by another's success. Perhaps to justify our personal failures or flaws, we magnify the past shortcomings of others. The more our jealousy grows, the more this demon exploits our thoughts, until *nothing* about the individual or his congregation seems right. In the final stage, we actually wage a campaign against him. No defense he offers will satisfy us. We are convinced he is deceived and dangerous, and we think it is up to us to warn others.

Yet the truth is that the person whose mind is controlled by the faultfinder demon is the one who is deceived and dangerous. His own unrepentant thoughts toward jealousy and fleshly criticism have supplied hell with a "lumberyard" of material to erect walls between members of the body of Christ.

Sadly, it is often leaders who fall from the intensity of their first love for Christ and become the fiercest persecutors of others who are seeking to possess more of the Holy Spirit. Christ's disciples will be persecuted, but I can find no biblical authorization for Christians to persecute others. Persecution is a deed of the flesh.

"But as at that time he who was born according to the flesh persecuted him who was born according to the Spirit, so it is now also" (Gal. 4:29). Incredibly, those who are given to persecuting others often actually think they are "offering service to God" (John 16:2).

To combat this enemy we must create an atmosphere of grace among us as individuals and between us as congregations. Like the Father who has given us life, we must seek to cause all things to work together for good. If one stumbles, we must be quick to cover him, without going so far as to create a false "cover-up" where we actually condone sin or hypocrisy. Yet, we proceed with the knowledge that we are "members of one another" (Eph. 4:25). As it is written, "None of you shall approach any blood relative of his to uncover nakedness; I am the LORD" (Lev. 18:6). We are family, begotten from one Father. "Their nakedness you shall not uncover; for their nakedness is yours" (v. 10). Even under the old covenant it was unlawful to uncover another's "nakedness" publicly. Love has eyelids as well as eyes. It covers a multitude of sins.

WHERE THE VULTURES ARE GATHERED

The accuser uses yet another weapon, and it uses this weapon astutely. There are times in our walk with God when, to increase fruitfulness, the Father prunes us back. (See John 15.) This is a season of preparation during which the Lord's purpose is to lead His servants into new power in ministry. This growth process requires new levels of surrender as well as a fresh crucifixion of the flesh. It is often a time of humiliation and testing, of emptiness and seeming ineffectiveness as God expands and deepens our dependency upon Him. It can be a fearful time when our need is exposed in stark visibility.

Unfortunately, not only is this time of weakness apparent to the man or woman of God, but it also frequently occurs before the

Church and before principalities and powers as well. The fault-finder spirit, and those who have come to think as it thinks, find in this pastor's vulnerability an opportunity to crush him.

Time and again, what would otherwise become an incubator of life becomes a coffin of death. Those who might otherwise emerge with the clarity and power of prophetic vision are beaten down and abandoned, cut off from the very people who should have prayed them through to resurrection. In this attack the faultfinder is most destructive. Here this demon aborts the birth of mature ministries, those who would arm their congregations and lead their church into breakthroughs.

The faultfinders and gossips are already planted in congregations —perhaps *you* are such a one! When the living God is making your pastor more deeply dependent, and thus more easily shaped for His purposes, do you criticize his apparent lack of anointing? Although he did not abandon you during your time of need, do you abandon him now when your faith might be the very encouragement he needs to yield to the cross?

Those who are sympathetic to the accuser of the brethren fulfill, by application, Matthew 24:28: "Wherever the corpse is, there the vultures will gather." The backbiting of these vulture-like individuals actually feeds their lower nature, for they seek what is dead in a congregation; they are *attracted* to what is dying.

Eventually these faultfinders depart, instinctively looking to take issue with some other congregation. "These are grumblers, finding fault…the ones who cause divisions" (Jude 16–19). They leave behind former brethren severely wounded and in strife and a pastor greatly disheartened. Soon they join a new congregation, and in time God begins to deal with this new pastor. Once again the faultfinder spirit manifests itself, strategically positioned to destroy another congregation.

Today God is seeking to raise up His servants with increased power and authority. In the pruning stage of their growth, will we water their dryness with prayer and encouragement, or will we be vultures drawn to devour their dying flesh?

HOW TO CORRECT ERROR

When the accuser comes, he brings distorted facts and condemnation. Those who are trapped by this spirit never research the *virtues* in the organization or person they are attacking. With the same zeal that the faultfinders seek to unearth sin, those who will conquer this enemy must earnestly seek God's heart and His calling for those they would reprove. True correction, therefore, will proceed with *reverence*, not *revenge*. Indeed, are not those whom we seek to correct Christ's servants? Are they not His possession? Is it possible the works of which we are jealous, and thus critical, might be the very works of Christ? Also, let us ask ourselves: Why has God chosen *us* to bring His rebuke? Are we famous and renown for loving people, or are we known as being judgmental and confrontational?

These are important questions, for to be anointed with Christ's authority to rebuke, we must be committed to men with Christ's goal to redeem. But if we are angry, embittered, or jealous toward another, we cannot even pray correctly for that person, much less reprove him. Jesus, the great Lion of Judah, was declared worthy to bring forth judgment by virtue of His nature: He was a Lamb slain for men's sin. *If we are not determined to die for men, we have no right to judge them.*

There are many legitimate, even healthy, reasons to switch congregations, and people should be free to fulfill their call as God leads them. Yet, those who seek to justify leaving a congregation should not do so simply through finding fault. Rather we should openly communicate with the ministerial team. Our attitude should be one of prayer and love, leaving a blessing for what we gained by our time spent there. If there has indeed been sin in the ministry, we should contact the church authorities in the city and leave the situation with them.

Additionally, local ministers and church members should be in communication with one another, never basing their opinion of another congregation or leader on the testimony of one who has just left it. If people start attending your congregation and bring with them a root of bitterness against their former assembly, that root will spring up in your congregation, and many will be defiled. Therefore, no matter how much your congregation may need new members, be cautious about building with individuals who are bitter or unreconciled to their former fellowship. It is wise to establish protocols between churches and create healthy avenues of communication so the process of movement can be a blessed transition and not an occasion for strife and dishonor.

Indeed, the Lord's word to us is that in the house of the Lord criticism must be replaced with prayer and faultfinding eliminated with a covering love. Where there is error, we must go with a motive to restore. Where there are wrong doctrines, let us maintain a gentle spirit, correcting those in opposition.

> *Dear Lord, forgive us for our lack of prayer and the weakness of our love. Master, we want to be like You, that when we see a need, instead of criticizing, we lay down our lives for it. Lord, heal Your Church of this demonic stronghold! In Jesus's name, amen.*

Twenty

God's Strategy for Our Cities

THERE IS ONLY one plan that will win our cities. God has it, and we must seek Him to receive it. Since Jesus already warned that "a house divided against itself shall not stand" (Matt. 12:25), the first strategy for the believing Church is that we be united. Then the outworking of our unity must result in the citywide church becoming in its own unique way a house of prayer. Emerging from Christ-centered unity and Christ-initiated prayer will be the Father's unique strategy for our cities.

GOD HAS A STRATEGY FOR YOUR AREA

Our confidence is that God does have a plan for our cities. Even as Christ did not operate out of a general benevolence toward men, only doing the things He saw the Father do, so we also must seek God until we are following His plan.

Whether we are aware of it or not, the Father always operates strategically in His affairs with men. Who among us has not stood in awe as the Lord orchestrated people, purposes, and events with eternal precision—a bill was paid, a word was spoken, we met the right person at just the right time? As the Father's wisdom unfolds, we will become increasingly aware that God is working continually on many levels. The seeming insignificance of our actions or prayers is part of a multifaceted strategy from the Most High, and those actions and prayers are an aspect in the overall success of His plan.

Therefore, whatever He says to do, no matter how small, we should do it, trusting in the greatness of His wisdom.

When Jesus sent the seventy disciples to drive out demons from men, Christ Himself was positioned in a higher realm, "watching Satan fall from heaven like lightning" (Luke 10:18). On one level, the disciples were warring against demons; on another, Jesus was warring against Satan, watching him fall like lightning.

Again, when Jesus sent out His seventy disciples, there was a divine wisdom governing their movement. The disciples were not traveling randomly about Israel. Rather, they were sent specifically to cities where Jesus would soon visit (v. 1). It was actually in context of being integrated into the overall strategy of God that Jesus gave His disciples authority "over all the power of the enemy" (v. 19). Their authority was not independent from obedience to Christ but because of it. It was a small part of a greater whole.

The disciples could not, as a rule, use their authority indiscriminately against the enemy the way Christians attempt to bind a principality today. No. They were united together under Jesus. He issued the commands and gave them authority in context with the commands.

OBEDIENCE, VIRTUE, AND POWER

"You are strong, and the word of God abides in you, and you have overcome the evil one" (1 John 2:14). To become strong like these young men John addressed, we must also abide in Christ's Word. The Word of God is a two-edged sword; that is, there are two aspects of the Word, each as sharp as the other. The first is the *established* will of God, which comes through knowing the Scriptures. The second is the *communicated* will of God, which comes through our relationship with the Lord.

Obedience to both dimensions of the Word is essential for our success. However, before God leads us to take our cities, He will inevitably lead us into the desert. Here, in a wilderness of weaknesses and temptations, obedience to each edge of the sword is tested and refined; here is where the power of God comes forth.

This time of testing may come to us as individuals, singular congregations, or as a citywide church. Regardless, we must pass God's tests before we graduate into power. Thus, our concept of being "Spirit-filled" must adjust to include this dimension of testing and warfare. In this hour many who are truly filled with the Holy Spirit will likewise find themselves facing battles that God has allowed to prove their character. The disciple of Christ should note carefully: our greatest spiritual growth occurs when no one is looking, when we feel even God has withdrawn from us.

We see both the pattern of God's dealings and the wisdom of His ways in Christ. "Then Jesus was led up by the Spirit into the wilderness to be tempted by the devil" (Matt. 4:1). Jesus had just been baptized by John when the heavens opened, and the voice of God audibly affirmed the Father's pleasure in His Son. We would expect that after this a glorious ministry would begin, but instead, Jesus was led by the Holy Spirit into a direct encounter with Satan in the wilderness. Here the very word the Father had spoken concerning Christ's sonship was tested by the devil.

Christians need to accept that the Father is not squeamish about testing His sons and daughters. The word *tempted* in this text means "proven or tested through adversity." God led Jesus *to be tested in spiritual warfare with the devil himself!* Mark's account adds that this happened immediately after the baptism of John and that Jesus was impelled into the desert by the Spirit; Luke's Gospel states that Jesus was "full of the Holy Spirit" during this test. This was not a matter of His flesh falling into temptation but His character being proven in temptation. Christ was tempted as we are (Heb. 4:15), in His mind, with weakness washing over His soul. To perfect character, the temptations we experience must be *real* temptations that lead us to *real* choices, which develop sustained character. The doubts must be legitimate questions; the fleshly temptations must have credible pleasures. Yet in the face of what Satan hurls, we must remain loyal to God.

The outcome of this testing was that "Jesus returned to Galilee in the power of the Spirit" (Luke 4:14). After success in warfare came a level of power that brought healing for every disease and illness. How exactly did Jesus receive power? He responded to the temptations of Satan with the established, written Word of God ("It is written"). Christ knew and obeyed the scriptural expression of God's will. However, the enemy countered by also using Scripture. At that point Jesus responded with "It is said." He knew and obeyed the *communicated* will of God (Luke 4:9–12).

We think of warfare in terms of "binding and loosing," but the endorsement of heaven, which actually accomplishes what we have decreed, is established in the wilderness of temptation and weakness. There is no authority without Christlike character, no lasting deliverance without facing the enemy and defeating him with God's Word.

Jesus lived by every word that proceeded out of the mouth of God, both written and spoken. In the overall strategy of God, this is central to His plans: that the Church, first of all, become Christlike. When we feel tempted and self-condemned, we must remember it is here, in this season of weakness, that character is developed and anointed power comes to deliver us from the devil.

Blessed Father, You are our strategy; You are our power. Grant us courage to overcome the enemy in spite of our weaknesses. For the sake of the multitudes who will experience Your anointed power upon us, grant us victory to obey You even when no one is looking. In Jesus's name, amen.

Twenty-one

It Takes a Citywide Church

M ANY CHRISTIANS BELIEVE that in the last days the only unity will be in the apostate church. Ironically, it is the very enemy they fear, the Antichrist, that has separated them from other born-again congregations in their city! Their aloofness is rooted in self-righteousness. Such an attitude cannot win the war for their cities!

UNITED IN WORSHIP AND WAR

One need not be a Bible scholar to recognize that the Jews had to be uncompromisingly united in their worship of God. All Israel was required to come to Jerusalem three times a year to worship during the feasts. If their worship was compromised, and they were serving the pagan gods of the region, they could not stand in battle. However, in addition to unity in worship, they also had to be united in warfare. Unless they ultimately faced the battle as "one man," their victory was rarely assured. (See Judges 6:16; 20:1, 8, 11; 1 Sam. 11:7; Ezra 3:1.)

From the beginning, the Lord has called us to be our brother's keeper. His standard has not changed. Today He is still calling us to cease fighting with one another and to unite in Christ against our common enemies.

There is an Old Testament story that reveals the heart we are seeking. The Israelites were in the land of Gilead about to cross the

Jordan River (Num. 32). The tribes of Reuben and Gad, which had amassed much livestock, asked that their inheritance be given first, as the land on which they stood was suitable for grazing. Their request angered Moses, for he assumed they sought to divide from the nation in order to gain their individual inheritance.

However, Reuben and Gad had a vision greater than Moses realized. Their words to Moses capture the attitude we must have concerning the other congregations in our cities. They said, "We will build here sheepfolds for our livestock and cities for our little ones; but we ourselves will be armed ready to go before the sons of Israel, until we have brought them to their place" (Num. 32:16–17). They refused to put down their swords until every tribe had gained its inheritance.

Truly, each congregation must maintain its individual "sheepfolds," the local fellowship, for the sense of family and continuity. We are compelled by God's love to provide a spiritual shelter to raise our "little ones." However, we must also be armed and ready to war on behalf of our brethren.

You see, although we are divided by "tribes" (denominations), we are all part of the same spiritual nation. And while we all have unique battles facing us, our collective and conscious unity under Christ's anointing brings terror to the heart of our enemy. It is this united house of the Lord that will turn our cities to God.

Consequently, in this hour God is raising up strong, seasoned leaders who are equipping their saints to pray and war on behalf of the *other* congregations in their city. Intercessors are being trained not only to protect and defend the citywide church but also to go before them to help secure their inheritance in Christ. Our prayer is that the attitude in Reuben and Gad will become the stance of the mature congregations in every city. They said, "We will not return to our homes until every one of the sons of Israel has possessed his inheritance" (v. 18).

Our Strategy in Spiritual Warfare

To go successfully before our brethren in war, the Lord Himself must prepare us. If we ignore the Lord's training, a confrontational posture against the enemy will be, at best, ineffective and, at worst, dangerous. If you attempt to "bind" the enemy but harbor sin in your heart, you will certainly be defeated. We have no authority over a foe *outside* of us if we are compromising with that foe *inside* of us. Thus, after discerning a ruling principality or power over an area, our first step in warfare is to cleanse the citywide church of its openness toward demonic influence. After pulling down the corresponding strongholds among the people (that is, repenting of the areas of our hearts that are similar to the enemy we are confronting), we then seek God in order to discern if this is an enemy He is calling us to confront.

Several years ago, when we were in the Washington DC area, the Lord revealed that we were to pray against the power of deceit over the area. Since deceit was also somewhat operative in the Church, our first act was to cleanse the participating congregations of deception. We did so by calling everyone to expose and confess their secret sins. After breaking the power of deceit over us, we prayed. That very evening, Marion Barry, the mayor of Washington, was arrested for drug use. The media reported that the police had sought his arrest for years, but he had cloaked himself "in deceit."

As in any war, many things must be in place before the Lord will engage the Church in confrontational warfare. We must not be anxious to try our new "doctrinal gun" of spiritual warfare, especially if our hearts are not filled with the firepower of Christ Himself.

More often, however, the Lord gives discernment, not for us to engage in warfare, but so that we will be aware of the enemy and be cleansed of his influence. In the initial stages of our training, we will soon discover that the Lord is more concerned with establishing His presence in the Church than He is with addressing the regional powers of darkness. It is not until the nature of Christ is in us and the voice of Christ is speaking through us that the Spirit of Christ penetrates the heavenly places, displacing the spiritual darkness over an area.

Suppose, however, that a number of congregations are participating and that you have repented and are cleansed of the influence of the specific enemy you seek to confront. How do you engage in warfare? The answer to this question is multifaceted. First, our prayers must be scripturally based expressions of God's *written* judgment as seen in the Scriptures. The "sword of the Spirit" is the "word of God" (Eph. 6:17). We must never boast about what we will do to the devil. We are servants carrying out God's will through speaking His Word.

Additionally, our prayers are not mere words without corresponding actions. Our prayer of judgment is a representation of our commitment to see the kingdom of God prevail in the very territory Satan held, even if it costs us our lives. In other words, our prayers are backed up by a willingness to die for what we believe.

Prayer is not our only weapon. Our feet are shod in preparation to speak the gospel. While we war in prayer, we are simultaneously reaching out to people through evangelism, seminars, and publications; through teaching on the radio and television; and, when appropriate, by participating in public demonstrations. You see, although our assault begins in the heavenly places, it extends to many fronts.

"BY MY SPIRIT," SAYS THE LORD

Jesus said, "If I cast out demons by the Spirit of God, then the kingdom of God has come upon you" (Matt. 12:28). The actual practice of waging spiritual war must be accomplished through the Holy Spirit. Jesus said the Spirit would "convict the world concerning sin, and righteousness, and judgment" (John 16:8). As individuals, the path of spiritual maturity begins with conviction of sin. It leads to our receiving Christ Himself as our righteousness. As Christ dwells within us, judgment is manifested against the enemy.

We must see that it is Christ in us who initiates our war against hell. Those who warn against immature Christians engaging in spiritual warfare are correct. To succeed, we must wage a *holy* war. As we have participated with the Holy Spirit in the transformation of our souls, so also are we joined with Him as He leads us into the unfolding stages of confrontational warfare.

Please also note that Jesus said the Spirit would "convict the world concerning sin." This is important. Judgment begins first with the household of God. However, the same Holy Spirit who has transformed us enlists us to transform society. And in His war against the devil, the same pattern that captured us is used against the world. Thus, the Holy Spirit brings conviction to a city; He establishes righteous attitudes in the soul of that city; and to the degree the community turns toward God, Satan is displaced in the heavenly places.

Therefore, as we discern the strongholds over our cities, we ask the Spirit to bring conviction to our society concerning these specific sins. During one of our city prayer times, we prayed that the Holy Spirit would convict drug dealers of sin. We even asked that He would make them fearful so they would come tearfully to God for help. A few days later I received a call from a man who had been selling drugs. He was crying, desperate and scared. He reported that a number of drug dealers in the city had similar feelings; some had even decided to take financial losses and leave. He himself had been a Christian and was backslidden. Today this man is a thankful member of our congregation. Now when he cries, his tears are tears of joy at the wonderful mercies of God.

Another time the Holy Spirit revealed that racism had created a stronghold of death in the black community. We began to take action on several fronts, including praying together with our African American friends and pastors. We even had a reconciliation service at our city hall that was attended by area mayors and police chiefs. The event was actually instrumental in leading our mayor and his wife to Christ. At the end of the televised meeting, we asked our brethren of color to forgive our long-standing abuse and prejudice. We then covenanted with God, as brethren joined together in Christ, that Cedar Rapids would be a "city of refuge" free of racism and cultural strife.

You see, we did not just pray about racism; we took steps to pull down this stronghold. The strategy is to pray, hear the Holy Spirit, and then act out what He reveals needs to change on a citywide basis. As a by-product, when the Rodney King riots broke in Los Angeles, it happened that in Cedar Rapids we had planned months earlier, on that very weekend, to unite in an interracial prayer walk and picnic. While the rest of America suffered under racial tension, we actually grew closer to one another.

You see, when the Lord builds the house, then the Lord will guard the city. The Lord had the antidote already planned before the "dis-ease" of rioting hit the nation.

We also pray for our civic leaders, that the Holy Spirit would bring righteousness into the thoughts and attitudes of the secular leaders. We intercede for governmental agencies to judge and act with righteous judgments, praying for specific individuals to come to know Christ. We pray the same way for the newspaper and local television. In that regard, we have seen the paper swing toward a more conservative profile. Do not just lament the condition of the communications media; intercede for them. The media have a strong influence over our cities, and they need our prayers.

Another phase or arena of warfare the Holy Spirit engages in is judgment: "because the ruler of this world has been judged" (John 16:11). It is part of the Holy Spirit's ministry to bring God's judgment against the powers of darkness. Satan has already been disarmed and rendered powerless, defeated at the cross of Christ (Col. 2:15; Heb. 2:14; 1 John 3:8). The Holy Spirit conveys this eternal reality, granting authority to the Church to establish God's will on Earth as it is in heaven.

Our churches used to be divided between charismatics and Baptists. One of the pastors with whom we pray felt the Lord wanted to bring healing between the Pentecostals and Baptists in town. Following his lead, we repented of spiritual pride concerning the gift of tongues, asking God to direct us to our Baptist friends. That very evening, as I was looking for a used computer to purchase, I responded to a classified ad in the paper. Although the man who had placed the ad introduced himself as a Baptist pastor, I had forgotten our morning prayer. The following morning I went to his house. After an hour or so of computer talk, I stood to leave. Suddenly, the Baptist pastor asked, "What is God doing?"

I finally remembered our prayer! Tears filled my eyes as the presence of the Lord entered the room. I told him that, just the day before, we had asked God to lead us, and that as charismatics and Pentecostals we had repented for allowing the gifts of the Spirit to divide us from other Christians.

"Wait!" he exclaimed. "I was just with the Baptist pastors in town telling them how we needed more of the gifts of the Spirit like the Pentecostals!"

The next week this pastor was united with us in prayer, and two weeks later we were praying with him at his church. In time he brought other Baptist pastors into our prayer fellowship. It is significant that the first pastor's name is Paul Widen, for we feel God surely wants to widen our vision of the Church.

This is the ministry of the Holy Spirit. Our warfare is never to be fought with human might or natural power. Only as the Spirit of the Lord works with us do we see the Church rebuilt and victory come. God wants us directed into Spirit-led prayer that confronts the strongholds of the city, utilizing the power of the Holy Spirit as our weapon.

DRY BONES OR A GREAT ARMY?

One obstacle we must overcome is the illusion that we, because of our ability to "divide the word," are more spiritual than other congregations. This delusion works on many churches concurrently and separates congregations throughout a city. Thus, we remain divided, isolated by our own spiritual pride. But as God delivers us from our arrogance, we see that we are without understanding when we compare ourselves to ourselves. We are not called to judge one another but to "love one another."

What God is doing today is much like the restoration of the Jews from their Babylonian captivity. Under the threat of warfare, and in spite of discouragement, the Jews were rebuilding the temple. Nehemiah instructed the workers to carry a building tool in one hand and a sword in the other (Neh. 4:17). If one section of the wall came under attack, a trumpet sounded, and all rallied to defend that area.

It must be the same for us. Many times the enemy has been able to defeat a particular congregation only because the rest of the citywide church was indifferent or unaware of the battle. In this context we must perceive that it takes a citywide church to win the citywide war.

I hear the reply, "The churches in our city are dead, and we alone are left." Such was Elijah's lament, but the Lord assured him there were yet seven thousand who were faithful. Ezekiel also thought he stood alone, but God brought him out to a valley of dry bones and commanded him to prophesy, to speak to those bones. *After* the bones came together, then the Spirit entered, and behold, they were "an exceedingly great army" (Ezek. 37:10).

One of the sins of the Church is that we criticize the dry bones, judging them for being lifeless. Yet we fail simply to *speak* to them. There are thousands of pastors and congregations who only need to be spoken to and connected with others in the body. God is indeed preparing an exceedingly great army. Through it He intends to pull down the strongholds in the cities. However, they must be *connected in Christ* before the Spirit will anoint them for effective spiritual warfare.

Please hear me. We thank God for national days of prayer and regional weeks of supplication, and we are calling tens of thousands to pray for specific areas to change. These strategies are essential for loosening the enemy's grip over an area. But if we want to see Satan's kingdom fall, the Church must be united. If the city church is bound and divided by strife, the enemy in that region will not be plundered.

When we pray against the spiritual forces of wickedness over a region, our first line of offense is to pray for the congregations to be united in their worship and their warfare. Why pray for the Church? Scripture tells us, "The adversary and the enemy entered the gates of the city because of the sins of the prophets and the iniquities of the priests" (Lam. 4:12–13, author's paraphrase). Indeed, if there is "jealousy and selfish ambition" in the Church, there will inevitably be "disorder and every evil thing" in that locality (James 3:16).

Therefore, we conclude: it takes a citywide church to win the citywide war. Our individual evangelistic programs, our Sunday teachings, and our aggressive attempts to bind the enemy are of limited value if we, the born-again Church, remain divided. One person's transformation from carnality to the image of Christ can revolutionize a congregation; the transformation of the citywide church into the image of Christ can revolutionize a city.

Let's pray.

Lord Jesus, forgive me for being so independent that I failed to see the needs of the other congregations in my city. You said that a house divided cannot stand. You also said that if we are not gathering with You in spiritual warfare, we are actually against You. Lord, I repent of being isolated. I ask You to equip me to be a strength and a help to my brethren throughout the city. Grant me grace, Lord Jesus, to fulfill this prayer to Your glory. Amen.

Twenty-two

The House of the Lord Is the Gate of Heaven

I N SPITE OF obstacles, occasional setbacks, and delays, there absolutely will be a people who take faith to see Christ-centered oneness with other Christians in their city. They will learn to appreciate their differences and honor one another as members of Christ's body. The world will know they are Christians because of their love.

We will attain such unity because our great ally in achieving our goal is the Lord Himself. It was foretold since ancient times that, at the end of the age, the Lord's house would be restored. Indeed, Isaiah tells us:

> Now it will come about that
> In the last days,
> The mountain of the house of the LORD
> Will be established as the chief of the mountains,
> And will be raised above the hills;
> And all the nations will stream to it.
>
> —ISAIAH 2:2

Isaiah 2:2 is coming to pass. Throughout the body of Christ, leaders and intercessors are uniting in unprecedented ways. Do not doubt, for the house of the Lord is being established. Even in spite of occasional setbacks, the trend is still toward unity.

How significant is this? In the history of the Church there has never been a time when Christians from so many backgrounds are seeking to remove divisions as we see today. The historic pattern of the Church has always been to divide from others and then criticize those with whom we once were associated. Yet today this trend is being reversed! Even when apparent conflicts arise, leaders are not allowing those divisions to become permanent. God is establishing His house.

Some would argue that this unity is a prelude to the "one-world church" of the Antichrist. Others contend that the emergence of the house of the Lord won't occur until after Christ returns. However, Isaiah plainly says that God's house will be rebuilt "in the last days."

The Book of Acts identifies the era that began at Pentecost as "the last days" (Acts 2:17). Thus, the time frame to which Isaiah's prophecy is referring is not the millennial age (although it will culminate in the Millennium), but it is being established during this present dispensation. I am amazed by the power in Isaiah's promise. He says that all nations "will stream...to the mountain of the house of the LORD." Only in God can streams flow up a mountain! This promise speaks of resurrection life being poured out upon the nations—drawing people out of the ancestral sins and generational curses that have, for so long, weighed oppressively upon them. Supernatural power is coming from God to reverse the gravity of life's situations and to create an updraft of hope and new beginnings!

Isaiah continues:

And many peoples will come and say,
"Come, let us go up to the mountain of the LORD,
To the house of the God of Jacob;
That He may teach us concerning His ways,
And that we may walk in His paths."

—ISAIAH 2:3

This too is happening in our day. While some may be focusing on the world and the frightening signs of the times, still others are seeking to go deeper: to learn God's ways and to walk in His paths. "For the law will go forth from Zion, and the word of the LORD from Jerusalem. And He will judge between the nations, and will render decisions for many peoples" (vv. 3–4). The Lord is rendering "decisions for many peoples" from His house. Beloved, it is the agenda of God to remedy the unresolved conflicts between us. He has decreed that racism and divisions cannot exist in God's house. As a result, reconciliation between denominations and races among born-again Christians has begun. Yes, there is still progress to be made concerning race issues; we must go beyond acceptance and truly embrace friendship. Blacks and whites must stand together and reach for the day when color will not trump love. Our prejudice must be for Christ to be exalted in each other.

As we remedy the ethnic issues of the past, the result will be: "And they will hammer their swords into plowshares, and their spears into pruning hooks. Nation will not lift up sword against nation, and never again will they learn war" (v. 4). What are "plowshares" and "pruning hooks"? They are instruments of the harvest. Swords and spears, once used against each other, are being retooled as we work side by side to reach the lost!

HOW AWESOME IS THIS PLACE

Yes, destructive judgments will come upon the world at the end of the age. Yet, an outpouring of redemptive mercy is also coming from the Lord; it is streaming through His house into the world. Yes, the Antichrist will arise, but so also will the glory of Jesus Christ be seen in His living house!

It is significant that Isaiah's prophecy refers to the Lord's house as "the house of the God of Jacob." It was Jacob to whom the first revelation of God's house came. We may think God should have chosen one more spiritual. Jacob was fleeing Esau, whom he defrauded. Yet, there is a message in this first unveiling of God's house: God chooses, redeems, and transforms whom He wills. (See Romans 9:18.) Those He draws into His house, He absorbs into His craftsmanship.

Let's look at this initial revelation of the house of God, for it speaks of the essence of what we will always find in this wonderful place. Jacob had stopped to rest. Putting his head upon a rock, he slept.

> He had a dream, and behold, a ladder was set on the earth with its top reaching to heaven; and behold, the angels of God were ascending and descending on it. And behold, the LORD stood above it.
>
> —GENESIS 28:12–13

The second characteristic of the Lord's house is this: it is the place where religion fades and the reality of God appears. This is where the living God has chosen to manifest Himself.

> Then Jacob awoke from his sleep and said, "Surely the LORD is in this place, and I did not know it." And he was afraid and said, "How awesome is this place! This is none other than the house of God, and this is the gate of heaven."
>
> —GENESIS 28:16–17

The Lord's house is "the gate of heaven." There is absolutely no place on Earth like the house of the Lord! It is truly an "awesome" place.

So Jacob called this angelic reality, this spiritual abode where God and man could dwell together, "Bethel," the house of God (Gen. 28:19). It speaks of more than the visitation of God; this is God's habitation.

THE HIGHEST PRIORITY

Throughout the Old Testament, it was the people's regard for the house of the Lord that revealed the condition of their hearts toward God Himself. Whether it was called the "tabernacle," "sanctuary," or "temple," God's house was the focus of His attention. Consider: by some counts there are fewer than ten chapters devoted to the entire Creation event, while more than eleven hundred references point us to the Lord's house. The construction and the service of the Lord's house clearly rise above all other themes in the Old Testament.

The house was to be a house of prayer, which would open the "gate of heaven." It was not only limited to Israel, but it was intercession that expanded "for all nations." In this place, sacrifice was brought; it was here that celebration was offered. Even in Israel's times of exile, the house was to remain their focused priority. The Lord told them that as they would "pray toward this place" (2 Chron. 6:20–21, 26), He would bring them back and "heal their land" (2 Chron. 7:14). In biblical times, revival was never consummated merely by an increase of miracles or signs. Supernatural wonders may have brought personal or localized revival, but only after the Lord's house was restored could national revival be attained.

One may argue that using the example of the Old Testament temple does not apply to New Testament Christians. Certainly, we are not seeking to rebuild the Jewish temple—although that would indeed be a revival of sorts. Our focus is not on a building made with hands but on the spiritual union created by believers united in Christ. Paul tells us that we are the temple of God, His living house. Thus, the principles that determined revival in the Old Testament are perfectly applicable to us in our times.

Today we are praying and working for revival in our land. If we would give the restoration of the Lord's house a higher priority...if we would repair our ruined relationships and rebuild our fallen unity…we would find an ever-increasing power from God to heal our national needs. We will never have the manifestation of heaven touch the earth without the restoration first of the house of the Lord, for God's house is the gate to heaven.

THE RIVER—KNEE-DEEP AND RISING

The prophet Ezekiel's words illumined what is about to occur. In chapters 40 through 43, Ezekiel foresaw a time when the house of the Lord would be rebuilt, returning God's glory to the temple (Ezek. 43:1–6). The following chapters continue speaking of the restoration, but then in chapter 47, Ezekiel records an amazing event: "From under the threshold of the house…from south of the altar," water was flowing (Ezek. 47:1). This water was but a trickle at first. Then it flowed ankle-deep, then knee-deep; soon it reached the loins and continued rising until it became a river that could not be forded. Ezekiel tells us that wherever the river went, it brought life and healing. (See Ezekiel 47:8–9, KJV.) It is important to see that the river did not flow straight from heaven; it came through the rebuilt house of the Lord!

Today the "river of refreshing" is beginning to flow in many parts of the world. It is not happening coincidentally but as a direct result of Christians coming together as the Lord's house. Now some will say, "Wait. The Church is not completely united. We still are divided in many ways." True. And others will say the river is still quite shallow. That is also true. We need to see that the depth of the river is proportional to the depth of our unity!

Just as the Lord is not done uniting us, so the river is not done rising. Imagine, therefore, what the river will look like when the Lord is finished building His house. Remember, in the last days this glorious house will be "established as the chief of the mountains" (Isa. 2:2). The house is the gate of heaven; the river runs through it.

Dear Lord, I long to see the house of the Lord established as "the chief of the mountains" and to see all the nations streaming to it. I want to go deeper, Lord, and to walk in Your ways. Teach me to go beyond mere acceptance of others who are "different" from me by denomination, culture, or ethnicity, and allow me and those in my family, community, and world to pick up our tools of harvest and bring the lost into Your house. May I never be content to plunge only ankle-deep into your river of refreshing, but lead me further in until I am knee-deep, waist-deep, and finally totally immersed in Your Spirit. Build Your house in me, and allow me to be a part of the "gate of heaven" leading others to Your life-giving river. Amen.

Chapter Highlights

PREFACE

- It will take the united effort of every Christian to win the citywide war against the powers of darkness. Our separate, isolated efforts will not stop the flood of increasing evil in our cities if we, as members of Christ's Church, remain isolated from each other.
- We have taken the liberty in this book to define the house of the Lord as that living, united, praying body of believers throughout the city where the many members of God's body become one. The Lord's house will consist of evangelicals and Pentecostals, liturgical churches and charismatics; it will be free of racial and class prejudices.
- Like all rivers, the eternal river of life avoids mountains. Yet it flows naturally into valleys and plains. Before we will ever be truly prepared for the Lord Jesus, the mountain of our pride must come down. It is a fact worth noting that, in preparation for Christ, God placed John the Baptist in the Jordan Valley. This valley is actually the lowest place in the world. The Lord began His greatest work in the lowest place on Earth. Indeed, all those whom the Lord empowers will pass through a valley of lowliness.
- God will give grace to the humble, and together they will bring a new purity to Christianity. They will speak with lasting credibility of Christ's forgiveness; they will be examples of His love toward one another.

CHAPTER 1

- Out of His desire to present a pure bride to His Son, the Father is purging the Church of its sin.
- Through new and successive levels of purity, the house of the Lord will again see and reflect the glory of God.
- God initiated His plan to redeem the nation by consecrating the priests and cleansing the Lord's house.
- Before the eternal One moves visibly in power, He moves invisibly in holiness.
- It is one thing for us to speak honestly with the Lord; it is quite another when He speaks without restraint to us.
- For us to become sensitive to divine realities, we must live with the door of our hearts open. It is impossible to do the will of God otherwise.
- We can be assured that each step deeper into the Lord's presence will reveal areas in our hearts that need to be cleansed.

CHAPTER 2

- There are costs to attaining God's best. If we want to have His greatest provisions, we must yield to Him our greatest loves.
- Even as the Lord carefully chose the building site for the temple of stone, so He is looking at the landscape of our hearts, seeking to make us His temple of flesh.
- Abraham's faith told him they would both return, but it was his attitude of worship that enabled him to go up.
- To qualify to be part of the house of the Lord, the first attitude we must possess is a worshiping heart; we must be willing to give to God what we love the most.

- Those whom God will use in building His house will be people who willingly surrender their greatest loves to God. Within their yielding, worshiping hearts, He will build His house.

CHAPTER 3

- If we will gain God's greatest blessings, we must embrace His highest purpose.
- If our goal is anything other than becoming a home for Jesus, this truth will become another "wind of doctrine"; we will be blown off course again. Without the abiding fullness of Christ in the Church, we will have no more impact in the world than a political party, whose strength rests in numbers and finances but not in God.
- We need to return to the simplicity and purity of devotion to Christ, and we desperately need divine intervention—or our nation will perish.
- We must abandon all hope of finding true spiritual success apart from dependent, steadfast faith in the person and power of Christ.
- We cannot attain to the works of God unless we first become the workmanship of God.
- Until we see that the Father's highest purpose is to reveal in us the nature of Christ, we will not qualify for the power of Christ, which is God's full endorsement upon our lives.
- We cannot see Christ corporately manifested in the Church until we, as individuals, embrace true Christ-likeness; nor can we plunder the heavenly places until we unite with other congregations as Christ's Church.

- It is the eternal wisdom and purpose of God to reveal Christ "through the church"—not only to the world but also to the "rulers and the authorities [principalities and powers] in the heavenly places" (Eph. 3:10).
- In battling for the soul of our cities and our nation, our victory is not in knowing how to command demons but in knowing the commander Himself. We triumph in being rightly aligned with the supreme plan of God, which is to fill all things with Christ.
- If we want to obtain the endorsement of God upon our lives, Jesus must become as real to us as the world was when we were sinners.

CHAPTER 4

- When pure Christianity degenerates into divided camps of ambitious people, it literally destroys the harmony, power, and blessing of the "temple of God."
- The living God is a God of order; He will not dwell in ruins! Because He is a God of love, He will work with us to rebuild, but He will not sanction our fallen condition with power. He will not lend His credibility to our disorder.
- Building the house of God—the born-again, praying, loving, citywide church—is still Christ's highest priority.
- The path narrows for leadership until our only choice is to become Christlike in everything.
- Consequently, the "disorder," lawlessness, and "every evil thing" we see in our society are, at least in part, rooted in the soil of a misdirected and distracted church community.

- Over the years the world has seen many incredible ministries. However, the time of the "incredible" has passed; the hour for the credible is being established.

CHAPTER 5

- We have instructed the Church in nearly everything but becoming disciples of Jesus Christ. We have filled the people with doctrines instead of Deity; we have given them manuals instead of Emmanuel.
- Three and a half years of undiluted Jesus will produce in us what it did in the disciples: the kingdom of God!
- The eternal One who established His kingdom in men two millennia ago is fully capable of producing it in us today. All we need is undiluted, uninhibited Jesus. All we need are hearts that will not be satisfied with something or someone less than Him.
- If we divide over forms of church government or peripheral doctrines, we will miss completely the true purpose of the Church, which is to make disciples of Jesus.
- After we recognize that the goal is not ministry but slavery, we will begin to see the power of Christ restored to the Church.
- The pattern for leadership in the years ahead is simple: leaders must be individuals whose burning passion is conformity to Jesus Christ.
- God can use practically any church structure if the people in that congregation are genuinely seeking Him.
- The outward form is not the issue with the Almighty; the true issue is the posture of the human heart before Him.

- Is it not true that the greater the sense of emptiness within us, the stronger is our hunger for God?
- Let us become people whose heart's passion is to seek God until Christ Himself is actually formed within us (Gal. 4:19).
- The Lord calls us to pay the same price, do the same works, and possess the exact same benefits from prayer that Jesus did.

CHAPTER 6

- Our call is to possess that love of God that reaches into eternity and brings the glory and person of Christ into His earthly house.
- In this maturation process there will come a point when, within your heart, love for God will take ascendancy over mere intellectual or doctrinal understanding.
- Genuine love for God is an unrelenting hunger.
- Let us also understand we will not find His fullness by seeking Him merely in convenient times and comfortable places. Rather, our quest is a determined, continual pilgrimage that will not end until He is disclosed to us. (See John 14:21; Philippians 3:12.)
- This is the greatest motivation for seeking the Lord: the time will come when you find Him!
- We all want the Lord, but only the bride will go so far as to find Him and bring Him back to the house.
- He sees your repentance as your preparation for Him— His bride making herself ready!
- We have many tasks, even responsibilities, which have come from heaven. However, the need of our soul is to be with Jesus.

CHAPTER 7

- It is possible for Christ's Church to be so properly aligned with heaven that the Holy Spirit actually displaces the powers of darkness over our cities.
- During these past years God has had His church "at the quarry," shaping the leaders and preparing their hearts to become part of the house of the Lord.
- Together with their congregations, these servants of God are building their congregations, not upon the typical American base of self-promotion and human enterprise, but upon a substructure of humility, prayer, and a commitment to Christian love.
- When the Lord builds the house, then the Lord will guard the city.
- Ultimately, how will the house of the Lord differ from current Christianity?
- Where the house of the Lord is built, the protection of the Lord will be felt.

CHAPTER 8

- The redemptive power of God is released when people forgive each other.
- Perhaps nothing so typifies the transforming, cleansing power of God as that which is experienced when a soul receives forgiveness.
- Whenever pardon is abundantly given, there is a definite and occasionally dramatic release of life against the powers of death in the heavenly places.
- Forgiveness is the very spirit of heaven removing the hiding places of demonic activity from the caverns of the human soul.

- The power released in forgiveness is actually a mighty weapon in the war to save our cities.
- Whenever any relationship exists outside the shelter of covering love, it degenerates into a system of mutual expectations and unwritten laws to which we all become debtors.
- Whenever we are unforgiving, we are also reacting. Those un-Christlike reactions to offenses become our sin before God.
- The redemptive plan of God was this: If the Israelites set free their slaves, they would not be taken as slaves. If they showed mercy, He would show Himself merciful as well. The destruction of their cities would be averted, for "mercy triumphs over judgment" (James 2:13).
- Any society that hardens its heart toward mercy opens its heart toward hell.
- Where there is a decrease of love, there will be an increase of demonic activity in our relationships.

CHAPTER 9

- There are things that make for peace. Pastors and their congregations must repent of the independence, spiritual pride, and insecurities that have kept them isolated from each other. God has wonderful, awesome plans for our cities. But the substructure of these "things that make for peace" is the citywide church becoming a house of prayer.
- The only way we can stand victorious before our enemies is if we kneel humbly before our Lord together.
- Even now, many large cities in the United States and Europe stand in the balance as to whether or not they

will turn toward God or become places of utter darkness, great despair, and destruction.

- God has placed the responsibility for our cities upon our shoulders!

CHAPTER 10

- Although calamities will become more devastating before the return of Christ, we must be assured of this: even in His wrath God is always remembering mercy. (See Habakkuk 3:2.)
- The righteousness and sanctification that the living Church produces in a society can literally preserve that society from much of the evil that might otherwise destroy it.
- We are not merely preparing for what is going to happen but who is coming. The bride is not making herself ready for a "date" but a marriage.
- The first phase of God's "vengeance" upon the world is aimed at releasing His elect from oppression.
- Whether it was with William Booth or John and Charles Wesley in England, Martin Luther in Germany, or Francis of Assisi in Italy, it has always been through the elect that the Lord has impacted and transformed society.
- The answer to the present condition in our nation is not new government programs or new policies, but it is New Testament Christianity—oaks of righteousness that are empowered with the redemptive mercy of God.

CHAPTER 11

- God does not hinder the healing of our land. Rather, our apathy and unbelief keep us from grasping the potential offered to us in the gospel of Christ. Do not marvel that entire cities can be saved. Scripture tells us that nations will come to our light and kings to the brightness of our rising (Isa. 60:1–3).

- Jesus spoke to entire cities and expected them to repent, and He expects cities today to repent as well.

- The strategy, therefore, to win our cities is for the Church to reveal Christ's life in power. Yes, the revelation of Christ in us as individuals and the power of Christ displayed corporately through us as His body can turn our worst cities back toward God!

- The sacrifice of Christ provides for the salvation of all men, and since the Father Himself desires all men to be saved, heaven waits only for the Church to act.

- You may say, "But that was then. Our cities are worse now. They are beyond redemption." Not so. Jesus continued His rebuke of cities by saying, "If the miracles had occurred in Sodom which occurred in you, it would have remained to this day" (Matt. 11:23). Amazingly, Jesus said even Sodom could find repentance!

- When we picture cities, we tend to see skylines and factories, streets and schools. Jesus, however, sees people.

- So much of our contemporary teaching keeps alive the very nature Jesus calls us to crucify.

- The Father's goal is not merely to bless us but to transform us into the image of His Son. He desires to use us to turn our families, communities, and churches back to Him. But God has made no provision for the healing of our land apart from the Church becoming Christlike.

- There is a legitimate dimension of faith that is coming from God. It is motivated by love and guided by wisdom, and it is coming from heaven to win the lost in our cities.

- Many Christians think knowing the promises is the same as obtaining them. True faith literally obtains the promises of God.
- If evil can enter our cities through our negligence, evil can be driven out through our diligence.
- You might ask, "But does this fit into my eschatology?" Our "eschatologies" can be an excuse for unbelief. The fact is that we do not know when Jesus is returning.
- Let us not look for the apostasy anywhere else but in our own hearts.
- In the midst of the most terrible of times, the greatest darkness, the Lord proclaims: "Arise, shine; for your light has come, and the glory of the LORD has risen upon you" (Isa. 60:1).

CHAPTER 12

- There are two Americas. One is indeed defiant and rebellious, constantly pushing the limits of morality. However, there is another America, a subset in society that does not make the news, nor does it embrace the wantonness of society.
- Because of the Christian seed in America, I do not see the United States being destroyed. However, I do see this nation facing severe chastening in the days ahead. The chastening will be deep and the blows mighty.
- When divine woundings come, remember God's hands also heal.
- Some think of America as a modern Babylon. To you I say that, even if we are exiled in Babylon, the command

is still to pray for the nation, for in its welfare is our welfare (Jer. 29:7).

- This interpretation by the early Church, that a great nation would be turned to God to protect the Church from persecution, offers a legitimate faith pattern for us. Consider this: the symbol of the United States is, in fact, the great eagle! And while we may argue about the future, let us acknowledge the past: the wings of this eagle have indeed provided refuge for persecuted peoples for hundreds of years!

- There is great spiritual wickedness in high places over America. Still, as wickedness has become increasingly more brazen over the last thirty years, so the true Church in the United States has become purer, with maturing prayer and unity.

- Despite all the flaws, prejudices, and injustices committed by Americans, there simply has never been a nation whose spirit was more given to protecting the Church, or people in general, than the United States.

CHAPTER 13

- The zeal that consumes us—as well as the love that compels us—is for our Father's house. Our goal, which we believe is God's goal, is to see the born-again Church functionally and relationally united under the blood of Christ.

- We believe God's purpose is not to break off national affiliations but to heal and establish relationships locally.

- In truth, our focus is not on becoming leaders but followers of Jesus; not on a new doctrine but on obedience to the directives of Christ.

- Religious pride was the first stronghold to fall, enabling us as pastors from different denominations to flow together. God help us that elitism not be the first sin to arise in this new stirring of God!

- If a congregation recognizes Jesus as Lord and sees the need to be spiritually reborn—if they hold to the truth of the Scriptures and long for the personal return of the Lord Jesus—then we receive them as our brethren.

- What is an "apostolic anointing"? In the same way a pastor is empowered by God to unselfishly care for his local congregation, so the apostolic anointing awakens local leaders to work together for the benefit of the expanded citywide body of Christ.

- Those building together are not intimidated by the strengths of our leaders. Rather, they appreciate and respect the diversity of ministry in the citywide church.

- Not out of corporate board meetings but out of corporate prayer and dependency upon the Lord came divine directives and ministry provisions for the Church.

CHAPTER 14

- The eternal foundation of the Church is the Lord Jesus Christ; we rest and build upon Him. It is wisdom to build the Lord's house with only Jesus in mind.

- We cannot separate what Jesus says from who Jesus is. Christ and His Word are one.

- Christ and His Word are inseparable. Jesus was not a man who became the Word but the eternal Word who became a man. His very core nature is the Word of God. And to reject or ignore what He says is to reject or ignore who He is.

- The building code of the kingdom must be obedience to the words of Christ.
- There is a storm coming; even now the sky has darkened and the first drops are falling. If we will endure, we must be built upon the rock. Please hear me: you cannot build your house in a storm. It is through the Spirit and words of Christ that the house of the Lord is built.
- When we seek to build upon a foundation other than Jesus, the results are everything but Jesus. Only Christ can create Christians.

CHAPTER 15

- The wisdom of God can take even a poor man, train him in the ways of the Lord, and give him a strategy to deliver a city.
- The chaos of our cities is not greater than the chaos that covered the deep, formless, pre-creation void. God's wisdom brought creation to order, and His wisdom can bring the Church back to order as well.
- What is "the fear of the Lord"? It is the human soul, having experienced the crucifixion of self and pride, now trembling in stark vulnerability before Almighty God.
- It is the awe-inspiring wonder of man living in fellowship, not with his religion, but with his God. In such a state the obedient man is invincible.
- The enemy does not fear the Church because the Church does not fear the Lord. As the fear of the Lord returns to us, the terror of the Lord will be upon our enemies.

- The Lord's house is built by wisdom. It is established as we compassionately seek to understand the needs of our brethren. After it is built and established, then knowledge fills the rooms with riches.
- Wisdom knows what to speak and when to speak it.
- Presented by itself, even knowledge about unity can be divisive.
- We can have all the right doctrines and still live outside the presence of God if our hearts are not right.
- The outcome of right doctrines is love—love that covers other Christians and builds up the body of Christ; it forgives when offended and serves without hidden motives. It goes extra miles ungrudgingly. If our doctrines are not producing this kind of love, they are a smoke screen that will keep us separate and outside the house of the Lord.
- Without knowledge we will perish, but knowledge without love is itself a state of perishing.
- To build the right foundation of the city church, therefore, we must all be in agreement about Jesus and His command to love one another. Greater wisdom than this will not be given concerning building the house of the Lord.
- Our labors must be for Jesus, not self. It must be the love of Christ that compels us, not a desire to rise in prominence among men.
- We must be more willing to serve than to lead, more willing to be corrected than to teach.
- True wisdom is not stubborn but is willing to yield to other ministries and perspectives. It must be unyielding in regard to the deity and centrality of Christ and yet fully aware that God desires all men to be saved.

- While the wisdom of God is meek, it is also "unwavering, without hypocrisy" (James 3:17). This is wisdom born out of vision, not organizational skills. It is unwavering because it sees that the builder of the house is Christ. It is genuine, "full of mercy and good fruits," overlooking mistakes, helping the weaker congregations, and disarming suspicion and fear with the credibility of Christ's unfailing love.

CHAPTER 16

- In a move of God some will be willing to die for what God is doing, and some outside it will be eager to kill them.
- Ultimately, the ability to discern whether a teaching is truly from God rests in our willingness to obey Him.
- In a move of God the gray routine of life ends. Both good and evil gravitate toward a state of fullness, stimulating prophets and "Pharisees" alike to their true natures.
- The "key" to unlocking the power of knowledge is obedience.
- It is to our shame that the devil desires men's souls more than the Church does. Therefore we must realize that revival will not sweep our land until we possess Christ's passion for the lost.
- One of our primary objectives in connecting congregations is that through our unity Jesus will be revealed. It is Christ's glorious presence in the Church, in contrast to the increasing darkness in our cities, that will draw multitudes to Him.

- The will of God is escorted to the earth through prayer. It is as simple as this: revival is an answer to prayer; if we do not pray, there will be no revival.
- The message that brings worldwide awakening is that which embodies what God is doing and proclaims what God is saying.
- A wonderful dawn is breaking upon the Church. While we have grown under the same teachers and fought against the same enemies, to our amazement we are discovering, in different ways, that the Lord has been guiding us all to Himself. This, we believe, is the anointed truth that God is speaking: It is time for the house of the Lord to be built. As Jesus steps forth from His house, I believe revival will break forth in many cities.

CHAPTER 17

- While the doctrines of Christianity can be taught, Christlikeness can only be inspired.
- The Church has many administrators, but few examples of Christ; many who can explain the doctrines of Christianity, but few who walk as Jesus walked.
- What is spiritual authority? It is nothing less than God Himself confirming with power the word of His servant.
- The Bible provides us with many examples of those with spiritual authority. Every example tells us the same underlying principle: those who are raised up by God are backed up by God.
- When the Church returns to teaching all that Jesus taught, our disciples will have authority to do all that Jesus did.

- Jesus lived in the deepest intimacies of the Father's love because He laid down His life for the sheep. If we will grow in true authority, we will do so by laying down our lives for His sheep.
- When we could easily fight and win, yet turn the other cheek; when we are unjustly opposed, yet quietly endure—at those moments spiritual authority is entering our lives.
- Jesus had a choice: legions of warring angels and immediate personal deliverance, or death on the cross and deliverance for the world. He chose to die for us. The willful decision to lay down our lives as Jesus did is the very path upon which true authority develops.
- Spiritual authority is the provision of God to transform the temporal with the power of the eternal.
- Divine authority requires divine sanction. This sanction comes from passing the tests of love.
- When authority is administered without love, it degenerates into control.
- We will walk in either the true authority of love, the false authority of control, or no authority at all.
- Since true authority is built upon love, its goal is to liberate, not dominate. Therefore, before one can truly move in spiritual authority, he must be delivered from fear and its desire to control; he must be rooted and grounded in love.
- God has given us people so we may train them, not merely count them. Of this group, those whom we inspire to live like Christ are actually the measure of our success, the test of our effectiveness in the ministry.
- As wide as our sphere of love, to that extent we have spiritual authority.

- The testing ground of all spiritual things is love, for love alone purifies our motives and delivers us from the deceitfulness of self.
- David gained the skills to slay Goliath, not on a battlefield, but by defending his father's sheep from vicious predators. He loved the sheep so much that he would even risk his life for them. So also we grow in authority as we protect our Father's sheep, the flock He has given us to love.
- Authority is muscle in the arm of love. The more one loves, the more authority is granted to him. If we love our cities and are willing to lay down our lives for them, God will enlarge our hearts, granting us authority to confront principalities and powers.
- If we are truly anointed in God's love, the price to see our cities saved is not too great, for it is the price love always pays: the willingness to die for what we care for.
- We have been in exile from the promises of God, but we are returning to rebuild the Lord's house. It is not a time to tear down the body of Christ; it is time to establish and to build up.

CHAPTER 18

- If the Lord would honor the dedication of the physical temple with a visible manifestation of His glory, how much more does He seek to reveal His glorious presence in His living temple, the Church?
- We also must be built together and "perfected in unity" if we would see the fullness of the Lord displayed among us and the world believe in Christ (John 17:23).
- The true house of the Lord is revealed when the Church, "without regard to divisions," is "fitted

together." Only then can the Church truly be unveiled as the temple of the Lord, "a dwelling of God in the Spirit."

CHAPTER 19

- More congregations have been destroyed by the accuser of the brethren and its faultfinding than by either immorality or misuse of church funds.
- In an attempt to hinder if not altogether halt the next move of God, Satan has sent forth an army of fault-finding demons against the Church.
- The faultfinder spirit's assignment is to assault relationships on all levels.
- Masquerading as discernment, this spirit will slip into our opinions of other people, leaving us critical and judgmental.
- If our thoughts are other than "faith working through love," we need to be aware that we may be under spiritual attack.
- What we do with what we see, however, is the measure of Christlike maturity.
- The enemy's purpose in this assault is to discredit the minister so it can discredit his message.
- To mask the diabolical nature of its activity, the faultfinder spirit will often garb its criticisms in religious clothing. Under the pretense of protecting sheep from a "gnat-sized" error in doctrine, it forces the flock to swallow a "camel-sized" error of loveless correction. (See Matthew 23:24.)
- The Church needs correction, and ministers and public leaders need accountability, but the ministry of reproof

must be patterned after Christ and not the accuser of the brethren.

- Even in the most serious corrections, the voice of Jesus is always the embodiment of "grace and truth" (John 1:14).
- To find an indictment against the Church, it is important to note the enemy must draw his accusations from hell.
- We cast down the accuser of the brethren by learning to pray for one another instead of preying on one another.
- We defeat the faultfinder when we emulate the nature of Jesus: as a lamb, Christ died for sinners; as a priest, He intercedes.
- With the same zeal that the faultfinders seek to unearth sin, those who will conquer this enemy must earnestly seek God's heart and His calling for those they would reprove. True correction, therefore, will proceed with reverence, not revenge.
- To be anointed with Christ's authority to rebuke, we must be committed to men with Christ's goal to redeem.
- If we are not determined to die for men, we have no right to judge them.
- In the house of the Lord criticism must be replaced with prayer and faultfinding eliminated with a covering love.

CHAPTER 20

- Emerging from Christ-centered unity and Christ-initiated prayer will be the Father's unique strategy for our cities.
- The Word of God is a two-edged sword; that is, there are two aspects of the Word, each as sharp as the other.

The first is the established will of God, which comes
through knowing the Scriptures. The second is the
communicated will of God, which comes through our
relationship with the Lord.

- The disciple of Christ should note carefully: our greatest
  spiritual growth occurs when no one is looking, when
  we feel even God has withdrawn from us.
- Christians need to accept that the Father is not squeamish about testing His sons and daughters.
- We think of warfare in terms of "binding and loosing,"
  but the endorsement of heaven, which actually accomplishes what we have decreed, is established in the
  wilderness of temptation and weakness. There is no
  authority without Christlike character, no lasting deliverance without facing the enemy and defeating him
  with God's Word.

CHAPTER 21

- Truly, each congregation must maintain its individual
  "sheepfolds," the local fellowship, for the sense of
  family and continuity. We are compelled by God's love
  to provide a spiritual shelter to raise our "little ones."
  However, we must also be armed and ready to war on
  behalf of our brethren.
- Although we are divided by "tribes" (denominations),
  we are all part of the same spiritual nation.
- We have no authority over a foe outside of us if we are
  compromising with that foe inside of us.
- In the initial stages of our training, we will soon
  discover that the Lord is more concerned with establishing His presence in the Church than He is with
  addressing the regional powers of darkness. It is not

until the nature of Christ is in us and the voice of Christ is speaking through us that the Spirit of Christ penetrates the heavenly places, displacing the spiritual darkness over an area.

- As God delivers us from our arrogance, we see that we are without understanding when we compare ourselves to ourselves. We are not called to judge one another but to "love one another."
- What God is doing today is much like the restoration of the Jews from their Babylonian captivity.
- God is indeed preparing an exceedingly great army. Through it He intends to pull down the strongholds in the cities. However, they must be connected in Christ before the Spirit will anoint them for effective spiritual warfare.
- It takes a citywide church to win the citywide war.
- One person's transformation from carnality to the image of Christ can revolutionize a congregation; the transformation of the citywide church into the image of Christ can revolutionize a city.

CHAPTER 22

- In spite of obstacles, occasional setbacks, and delays, there absolutely will be a people who take faith to see Christ-centered oneness with other Christians in their city.
- The historic pattern of the Church has always been to divide from others and then criticize those with whom we once were associated. Yet today this trend is being reversed!
- Only in God can streams flow up a mountain! This promise speaks of resurrection life being poured out

upon the nations—drawing people out of the ancestral sins and generational curses that have, for so long, weighed oppressively upon them.

- It is the agenda of God to remedy the unresolved conflicts between us.
- The Lord's house is "the gate of heaven." There is absolutely no place on Earth like the house of the Lord! It is truly an "awesome" place.
- In biblical times, revival was never consummated merely by an increase of miracles or signs. Supernatural wonders may have brought personal or localized revival, but only after the Lord's house was restored could national revival be attained.
- We will never have the manifestation of heaven touch the earth without the restoration first of the house of the Lord, for God's house is the gate to heaven.
- Today the "river of refreshing" is beginning to flow in many parts of the world. It is not happening coincidentally but as a direct result of Christians coming together as the Lord's house.

How Church Unity Has Impacted Cedar Rapids, Iowa

THIS APPENDIX WILL briefly outline our journey. Hopefully, it will inspire you to work toward greater unity with other congregations in your city.

In 1981, as a result of two pastors agreeing to meet over lunch to quench rumors about each other, the charismatic and Pentecostal congregations in our area began gathering monthly for prayer and fellowship. The pastor facilitating this ministerial prayer meeting was Charles Daugherty, from Fellowship Christian Center. In the mid-1980s, Charles stepped aside for personal reasons, and the monthly prayer ceased for nearly a year. The fellowship and prayer were greatly missed, and two other pastors, Gary Jenkins from First Assembly and Francis Frangipane, decided not only to rekindle the initiative but also to move their meeting to weekly.

These men not only invited the ten or so other pastors, but they also selected church intercessors and other city ministries to join them. This phase of the citywide prayer had a fluctuating group of about forty to fifty committed leaders and intercessors. Prayer began at 8:00 a.m. (later changed to 7:00 a.m.) in a rotating schedule that included each of the pastors' churches. After prayer, the host church provided a breakfast snack around which pastors and intercessors had fellowship. This morning prayer has continued to this day and has been led for most of that time by Duane McLean, an elder and pastor of intercessors at River of Life Ministries.

In the late 1980s, however, the pastors decided they needed additional time where they could express their needs more privately to one another. They also wanted to seek God for various citywide events, so a second prayer front opened Tuesday afternoons that was dedicated primarily to pastors and ministry leaders.

In 1991, after several years of unity, pastors from Pentecostal and charismatic traditions realized that one of the stumbling blocks hindering a greater unity between them and evangelical congregations was pride concerning spiritual gifts. We met with local Baptist pastors and asked them to forgive us for our pride. As a result, the Baptist pastors responded by asking forgiveness for a condescending attitude they had carried toward charismatics and Pentecostals. A healing process began between these two groups.

In 1992, seeking to expand the unity, white and African American pastors in the city met together to bridge the division that existed between them. White pastors asked their African American brethren to forgive them for the sins of racism, prejudice, and insensitivity, which had permeated the white culture. The African American pastors asked for forgiveness for the lack of trust and unforgiving attitudes they had held toward whites. This process of reconciliation was consummated in a public covenant made at city hall with various area mayors and police chiefs, and with full and positive media coverage.

As a result of this racial reconciliation, many good things have happened. The mayor of Cedar Rapids came to Christ. A few months afterward, another prayer front was opened at city hall, hosted by the mayor, at 6:00 a.m. From the time of this weekly prayer initiative forward for the next thirty months, there wasn't a murder in the city, even though a new mayor was in office over the last twelve of those months.

The city enjoyed concerts of prayer that were held at city hall and other churches. In February of 1992 we scheduled a prayer walk and picnic for the spring as a time to celebrate our racial diversity. It happened that, on the very weekend our event was to occur, the Rodney King riots broke out in Los Angeles, setting race relations back in many cities. However, in our community we made progress racially!

Additionally, the mayor and his wife began to travel with Pastor Frangipane to share their testimony of what the Lord Jesus was doing in Linn County. First Light, a ministry of reconciliation and love, also began, headed by Rufus and Betty Johnson. Each month churches from the black and white communities, as well as many other congregations from varied backgrounds, would host a meal and fellowship, leading to an increasing sense of brotherhood and family among the pastors of different ethnic and denominational backgrounds.

1998 TO 2003

In the late 1990s, Charles Daugherty returned to active ministry in Cedar Rapids, and in February of 1998, we made a decision to be strategic and intentional about growing the pastors' prayer group, with Charles serving as the facilitator. The gathering soon became a group of forty pastors who were hungry for fellowship and support. Our purposes have always included prayer and support for each other, our marriages, our families, our ministries, and especially for the lost. Charles will take the account from here.

Midwest CityReacher School

In August 1998, we hosted a regional CityReaching conference, with three keynote speakers from diverse backgrounds: Paul Cedar—president of the Evangelical Free Church and president of the Mission America Coalition; Ed Silvoso (Argentina)—Harvest

Evangelism; and Claude King, a Southern Baptist. Attendees came from Iowa and seven surrounding states. God was changing our internal culture.

Convoy of Hope

In February of 1999, thirty-five pastors began praying over a proposal to bring Convoy of Hope International to Cedar Rapids. God's answer was yes. Instead of the usual single host church for a Convoy event, thirteen local pastors signed the agreement to participate with their congregations. Convoy happened in October with a tent city that included a kids' zone, medical tent, dental tent, community services tent, free haircut tent, hospitality tent, and more than 40,000 pounds of groceries to give away. We had 1,500 people volunteer to help, and more than 3,500 people attended. The services offered included 650 medical screenings, 350 dental screenings resulting in 175 people who were placed in free dental programs, 450 free haircuts, and 200 résumés that were processed for employment. Many individuals came to a saving knowledge of Jesus as the Christ.

Banquet of Hope and Tree of Hope

One month following Convoy of Hope, we provided a full Thanksgiving dinner for six hundred honored guests. We took the names of our guests, children, and three items they would like for Christmas. In December, teams of two visited each home and personally delivered the gifts to the families. In October of 2000 we did it all again!

The Marriage Agreement

In January 13, 2000, 81 pastors and professional counselors signed a Marriage Agreement. By August the partners signing had grown to 104. At the end of three years, the State of Iowa published statistics showing that although marriage was down in the state, in

Linn County marriage had increased by 5 percent. In the state, the divorce rate had increased, but in Linn County we had a 15 percent decline. A total of 105 pastors and counselors "re-signed" in 2003.

Voices of Hope Patriotic Concert

In 2002, our community had a large two-week celebration that ended on July 4, called *The Freedom Festival*. As a result of that, our music ministry team initiated a God-honoring patriotic concert, held over two nights. It was an instant success.

SERVE THE CITY RESOURCE GROUP, INC. (STC)

From 1998 through 2000, God blessed us beyond our expectations. We found that we were not prepared to handle the blessings—our nets were breaking, so to speak. We were also pretty tired. The decision was made that we would hold off on any more large initiatives until we had a strategic plan in place and a team to support the plan.

In 2003, we drafted a thirty-five-page document addressing our intention to "reach our region" for Christ. We developed an action-oriented plan to get out of our seats and into the streets! STC is a 501(c)3 entity. We are a *group* of ministries agreeing to bring our *resources* together to *serve the city*.

We knew that to be successful in our desire to work together to "go," we would need to draft a mission and vision document, stating that it would take a citywide church to win the citywide war. We needed a plan that would provide the framework and process for a full city-reaching course of action. Within this comprehensive plan there would be support for tactical partial city efforts as well. We became convinced that these efforts would have more success if they were supported by a much larger vision and personal connections.

This strategy is the ongoing process of mobilizing the *whole body of Christ* in a geographically identified area. We want to strategically focus all of our resources on reaching *the whole city* with *the whole gospel*, resulting in the redemption of society and transformation of the city.

MISSION, VISION, AND CORE VALUES

Mission

The mission of Serve the City is to visibly demonstrate the love of Christ to the Greater Cedar Rapids area through collaborative prayer, care, and share efforts.

Vision

Our vision is to pray for, care for, and sensitively share the gospel with every man, woman, and child in the Greater Cedar Rapids area.

Our goal is to have:

- Every evangelical pastor in our area connected in a prayer and/or support group of some kind
- Prayer ministries with a connection for community-wide prayer initiatives
- Marriage and family ministries flourishing in each congregation and connected area wide
- Youth ministries impacting every middle school and high school, winning and discipling teens to Christ
- The majority of congregational and ministry leaders attending monthly LCAE luncheons
- Area compassion ministry teams meeting needs in our communities
- Campus ministries functioning in such a manner that every campus has a faithful witness to the Lord Jesus Christ

- All the rest of the ministries evident in the Greater Cedar Rapids area-wide church collaborating in such a way that our Lord will be pleased and the community would be blessed

Values

We have seven core values that guide what we do, how we plan, and how we relate to each other and our community. They are:

1. Christ centered
2. Congregational based
3. Community focused
4. Collaborative approach
5. Servant attitude
6. Cultural transformation
7. Sustainable pace

Strategy

We have established a working partnership with the Mission America Coalition (MAC) that includes coaching, being a pilot city, and conferences. We have structured ourselves around the MAC prayer, care, and share CityReaching initiative.

Important guiding principles

A lifestyle and not only an event—Some of us are very good at putting on events, but events are only one step en route to transformation.

A culture and not a program—We simply cannot change the world's culture if we are unwilling to change our own culture within our four walls. We must change our own church culture as individuals, families, and congregations.

We need to be continually asking: What can we do together that we cannot do alone? What can we do better together than we can do alone?

Jesus tells us that we must deny "self," which includes *self-interests*. When we study the Scriptures, we find the disciples moved from arguing about "Who is the greatest?" to actually defending one another in the Book of Acts! They moved from the *unholy trinity* of me, myself, and I to using words such as *we, our, us,* and more.

The rebuilding of the wall of Jerusalem in Nehemiah's day gives us an important picture for relating together today. More than forty distinct family units were named, and each family unit had a specific task to do. Unless they joined their work together, all efforts would be for nothing. They were to help each other if one unit experienced difficulty. Because they did this, they accomplished half the work in fifty-two days, working together under a strategic whole city, whole church plan.

STRATEGIC RELATIONSHIPS THAT HAVE RESULTED

Since 1998 we have co-labored in more than fifty "together" activities.

2007—Operation Serve

This CARE effort included more than fifty projects on thirty school campus locations in five school districts. More than four hundred volunteers from twenty-seven congregations stepped up to do the work of painting, roofing, weed whacking, leaf raking, gardening, using chain saws, and more. This resulted in more than sixteen hundred hours of free labor for the schools. We had eighty-four other people packaging 14,572 meals, which we sent to Nicaragua (flood crisis), as well as seventy-one people who stopped at the blood drive to donate! By being intentional, each work site was served by three or more congregations—thus presenting in a visible way our unity in Christ.

The flood of 2008

Early in June, a devastating flood hit Cedar Rapids. The National Weather Service called flooding in the city a "historic hydrologic event," as the swollen river poured over its banks at five-hundred-year levels. Linn County Sheriff Don Zeller said, "We're just kind of at God's mercy right now…we're going to need a lot of prayers."*

On Monday, June 9, Serve the City received a telephone call at 6:00 p.m. The caller knew what we had done in the past and knew our capabilities. His message was clear: "Can you help?" By the end of the next day, more than one thousand volunteers had gone door to door to give evacuation notices to more than two thousand homes.

Over the next twenty-five days, more than four thousand volunteers filled sandbags, delivered materials to emergency shelters, maintained water and food distribution centers, delivered nearly one thousand meals a day, moved furniture, delivered medications to clinics, and supported the shelters. Volunteers were deployed hour after hour to fill so many needs. We continue to serve as a contributing partner in the Linn Area Long-Term Recovery Coalition.

Eight Days of Hope

Four months after the waters receded, we were able to host the disaster response team of Eight Days of Hope. Due entirely to our participation in the response phase of the flood, we were able to work with the city and the six electrical, mechanical, and plumbing boards to craft a proper ordinance to allow Eight Days volunteers to serve in our community. Nine hundred seventy-two volunteers came from forty-one states and four Canadian provinces to serve

---

* Associated Press, "Flooding Hits Historic 500-Year Level in Iowa," FoxNews.com, June 12, 2008, http://www.foxnews.com/story/0,2933,365943,00.html (accessed January 15, 2009).

our community. Five hundred seventy-six Linn County volunteers stepped up. There were 40,419 man-hours expended, which resulted in $1.7 million of volunteer labor! We worked in 120 homes and completed 302 projects.

Hard Work

Serving others is hard work, and you prepare for victory in the off-season when no one is watching. Will you pay the price? Are you ready?

—Charles Daugherty

For more information, see www.servethecity.org.

In Christ's Image Training Institute

THE VISION

In 1970 the Holy Spirit gave Pastor Francis Frangipane a vision that included a powerful promise from Isaiah 60:2–3. The Lord warned, "For behold, darkness will cover the earth, and deep darkness the peoples." Yet, in spite of the increased advances of hell, the Holy Spirit also promised, "But the Lord will rise upon you, and His glory will appear upon you. And nations will come to your light, and kings to the brightness of your rising."*

The plan is the same as what compelled the first-century Church: *we are seeking to possess the character and power of the Lord Jesus Christ.* Whether your desire is to see your family transformed or your nation in revival, today is not the time to despair, but to prepare.

IN CHRIST'S IMAGE TRAINING

Our vision is to see hundreds of thousands of intercessors and pastors—as well as people from all walks of life—focus their energies on becoming Christlike. In Christ's Image Training (ICIT) provides two levels of foundational teaching, plus an annual on-site seminar and an opportunity to join Advancing Church Ministries Association.

Level I offers a six-month training opportunity. Each week two teachings will be sent to you via e-mail. Accompanying these uniquely selected teachings will be thirty-nine audio teachings on twenty-four CDs. Level I training focuses upon the vision of attaining Christlikeness, with added tracks on humility, redemptive intercession, and commitment to unity in the body of Christ.

---

* See Pastor Frangipane's book *The Days of His Presence* (N.p.: Winds of Fire, 2002).

Level II, Growing in Christ, is a three-month training program. This material introduces other national leaders with Pastor Frangipane. These are men and women who have been anointed by God for this season of harvest and represent a variety of ministry expressions. Such diversity helps acquaint the student with individuals who share the Christ-centered values esteemed in Level I. In the Level II material, ICIT students will experience the thoughts and passions of prophetic, evangelistic, and other ministry strengths and callings.

Whether your goal is to respond to God's call for full-time ministry or to become a radiant witness for Christ to your family, neighborhood, school, or workplace, ICIT offers training, spiritual impartation, and certification.

TESTIMONIES

We have received hundreds of wonderful testimonies from students of our In Christ's Image Training, and we want to share a few with you:

> The students in my group are being profoundly impacted by the course already. Most of them have been saved for decades, and yet they realize how much they still need to learn and do to be Christlike. ICIT is truly appropriate for the present Church and for these times. Thank you for your servitude and your faithfulness.
>
> —Scott M.

> My wife, two friends, and I completed the ICIT Level 1 training earlier this year. The teachings were powerful, especially as the Holy Spirit used them as catalysts to break strongholds and to expose our sinful natures.
>
> —Kevin

I'm already astounded at "new thought" patterns I'm developing. I've been waiting for the Rapture instead of working for the harvest—now my WHOLE mind-set has changed.

—Pastor Carol

It has been life changing. It has been a process of impartation that has caused my old roots to be dealt with and new ones to be planted instead. I never thought the training of the Holy Spirit would be so real and life impacting through this course when I first enrolled. I was just so desperate for Jesus Himself that I felt I had to do it. Now I know it has been God Himself who orchestrated my circumstances in order to fulfill His main passion for my life to see the emergence of the life of Jesus Christ in me. Praise the Lord!

—Steven H.

I was born again, loved God, and was serving in a ministry. But I was never "in love" with Jesus until Francis and ICIT entered my life and trained me in Christlikeness. Then something happened between Jesus and me. Everything is different now. And everything seems to make sense now (why we do the things we do as Christians). I no longer have to do things just out of a sense of obligation, but my understanding is being progressively opened up. Finally, I feel like I have seen His heart and felt it beat in me.

—Lynn O.

When I first began the ICIT course online, everything on the "outside" of my ministry looked good, but I knew I was in trouble in my own life. God used this course to touch many of the things inside me—so much so that I went to the desert for a month of prayer and fasting! During that time the Lord stripped me layer by layer of everything that had been killing me. He stripped me until all that was left was Jesus and me—totally exposed to each other. This saved my life and ministry.

—R. S.

ICIT is an answer to a prayer I've prayed for years. My husband and I have been part of the leadership of our congregation for more than fifteen years. During those years, difficult situations occurred, and I had a very hard time dealing with some of the things that we had to go through. When we were going through ICIT, I kept saying to myself, "Praise the Lord, *it* happens to others as well." Since we've *graduated*, I have gone back over the material when situations have arisen, and it has really helped me overcome and deal with things better. Thank you for your ministry.

—MARIE M.

I wish I would have had this class forty years ago. God has changed me more since I started this class than in my previous forty years as a Christian.

—A CALIFORNIA STUDENT

Resources

Mission America Coalition
P. O. Box 13930
Palm Desert, CA 92255
Phone: (760) 200-2707
Fax: (760) 200-8837
Web site: www.missionamerica.org

National Pastors' Prayer Network
c/o Pastor Phil Miglioratti
1130 Randville Drive 1D
Palatine, IL 60074
E-mail: phil@nppn.org
Web site: www.nppn.org

Serve the City
P. O. Box 11333
Cedar Rapids, IA 52410-1333
Phone: (319) 378-0337
E-mail: info@servethecity.org
Web site: www.servethecity.org

Advancing Church Ministries
P. O. Box 10102
Cedar Rapids, IA 52410

PROCLAIM HOPE!
P. O. Box 770
New Providence, NJ 07674
Phone: (908) 771-0146
Web site: www.proclaimhope.com

PROCLAIM HOPE!

PROCLAIM HOPE! serves the Church through a host of creative approaches designed "to proclaim the full extent of Christ's supremacy and to empower others to do the same." Each ministry focuses on fostering and serving a nationwide Christ-awakening movement, the God-given hope for which multitudes are praying around the world.

Out of decades consulting with a broad spectrum of Christian leaders from every stream of the Church, PROCLAIM HOPE! offers: Christ Awakening Rallies, Christ Roundtables, Christ Summits, Christ Colleges, CHRISTFests, and much more. Each initiative is meant to encourage a lasting, sustainable "Christ-awakening movement," especially among communities of congregations within cities and regions. It also gives high priority to training leaders (clergy and lay) in order to equip them to strengthen this movement where they live.

Founder David Bryant serves as lead facilitator for PROCLAIM HOPE! Formerly a pastor, minister-at-large for the InterVarsity Christian Fellowship, and chairman of America's National Prayer Committee—as well as the author of popular books on missions, prayer, and awakenings—David founded Concerts of Prayer International in 1988. Based today out of metro New York City, much of his teaching and training continues to draw on years of traveling the Church internationally. Currently, one strategic tool for spreading his vision is David's latest book: *Christ Is ALL! A Joyful Manifesto on the Supremacy of God's Son*.

Visit www.ProclaimHope.com and www.ChristIsAllBook.com.

A Place of Protection in Life's Storms

In *The Shelter of the Most High* Francis Frangipane gives trustworthy biblical evidence that in the midst of all our uncertainties and fears, there is an available shelter from God to shield us. Once you've found this place, nothing you encounter can defeat you. From wherever you are, you can reach—and remain in—the stronghold of God.

Visit your local bookstore

10814

CHARISMA
HOUSE
www.charismahouse.com